The
BACKYARD
HOMESTEAD

footprint
SMALL
PRESS

STEP-BY-STEP GUIE TO START YOUR OWN SELF
SUFFICENT MINI FARM ON JUST A QUARTER ACRE

The Backyard Homestead

Step-By-Step Guide To Start Your Own Self-Sufficient Mini Farm On Just A Quarter Acre

Small Footprint Press

declared or implied. Readers acknowledge that the author is not engaged in the rendering of legal, financial, medical or professional advice. The content within this book has been derived from various sources. Please consult a licensed professional before attempting any techniques outlined in this book.

By reading this document, the reader agrees that under no circumstances is the author responsible for any losses, direct or indirect, that are incurred as a result of the use of the information contained within this document, including, but not limited to, errors, omissions, or inaccuracies.

CONTENTS

INTRODUCTION

"There are no gardening mistakes, only experiments."

— Janet Kilburn Phillips

Are you looking for a change? Do you love gardening, or maybe even just like it a little bit but want to take it to the next level? Are you sick and tired of feeling dependent on a system that is becoming increasingly confusing and expensive? Maybe you are just looking to take more control over your own life and want to make the world a little bit better? Well, you've come to the right place! Our goal here at Small Footprint Press is to help you sustainably survive and thrive while ensuring together that the world is a better place for future generations to come.

Born out of frustration with the planet's current state, we want to raise awareness about how we all affect the world we live in and what you can do yourself & collectively to make a real difference.

We know how important it is to start giving back to the earth and how true happiness can come from living sustainably. Furthermore, having our own backyard homestead is an incredible way to put your worries to rest and mitigate many of the risks associated with potential catastrophes to come.

That's why we've taken the time to make sure that you feel safe and empowered in your own journey to sustainability. As the world gets more confusing each day, we are determined to keep life simple and ensure that everyone has the ability to survive off their own, homegrown food, no matter what situation they may face.

This book is going to teach you everything you need to know about sustainable living, growing your own food, and good old-fashioned homesteading. From personal preparation to prepping your land, understanding preservation, raising animals, and even making a profit, we are here to teach you everything you need to know to start homesteading this season.

The only thing you need to have before you start living sustainably is commitment. Homesteading can be hard work, so it is crucial to make sure you are physically and mentally prepared before you begin. Knowing the obstacles you may have to face and the benefits can help you better prepare for the commitment to farming your own homestead.

Planning a proper budget and finding the right space for your different crops is essential before you actually begin any of the real work. This book is going to teach you everything you need to know to get started and prepare you mentally for the tasks ahead.

Once you are ready to start, you also need to make sure your land is ready! Prepping things like garden spaces and structures, fences and pens, even plumbing or irrigation systems will be necessary for certain elements. In order for your homestead to succeed and thrive, you want to make sure you have all the proper equipment and all the right knowledge on how to care for each aspect of your new project. Luckily, we have all the info you need right here, just waiting for someone like you to get started! When it comes to gardening, prepping your space is half the work, which is why we've created this comprehensive guide that will teach you everything you need to know from start to finish.

Here at Small Footprint Press, our number one priority is mitigating your risks of potential disasters while taking care of the earth, which is why sustainability is so important to us. This guide will consist of all the most up-to-date information on sustainable farming and teach you how to do it yourself. You'll learn all the principles and goals for sustainable homesteading, as well as all the tricks to make sure you are as environmentally conscious as possible while working on your homestead. Homesteading is all about making use of what you have and using everything so that you leave little to no carbon footprint.

After you've grown your crops, though, you're going to need to know how to preserve them. Not to worry; we are here for you once again! On top of teaching the important information on preparing and growing your homestead sustainably, we will also provide you with the knowledge of how to preserve your yield. This includes everything from drying and smoking meats, to canning your fruits and veggies, and other options for keeping your produce fresh. There are so many small ways you can live more sustainably by turning common household objects into useful items for your homestead.

Once you get started on your homestead, watch how your life changes for the better; not only directly through the knowledge and pride you will get from growing your own food, but indirectly as well. A sustainable mindset can be applied to every aspect of your life, and we are prepared to help you with that, too. Incorporating animals such as chickens, goats, or even bees can take your homestead to the next level. Even things as simple as an optimized composting system can make your life so much easier and help reduce your impact on our planet.

Finally, we know that tending to your homestead requires a lot of intense effort and that it can take up a lot of your time. That's why we will also teach you some tips and tricks on how to profit off of all your hard work! From selling jam and jelly to handmade soaps and lotions to honey and beeswax, our book will give you some great ideas on how your homestead can start working for you, too. You should be able to enjoy all your hard work and have it pay off in a tangible way that can support you so you can get back to living your best, most sustainable life.

By the time you finish reading, you will have all the knowledge you need to start your own homestead, right in your backyard! Don't stress yourself out by worrying about whether or not you can do it or if you will succeed. Just try! There is never success without first failing at least a dozen times, in a dozen different ways. This is especially true when it comes to homesteading. You will only get better through doing, so even when you mess up or make a mistake, keep trying. There will always be new goals for you to reach and new opportunities for you to improve. Homestead-living is all about taking life as it comes, challenges and achievements, hardships and windfalls, obstacles and opportunities.

The No. 1 priority of this book is to help you get the information and tools you need to start living off the land and sustain ably right now. Our goal is to make sure you are living your best life while helping promote environmental consciousness and eco-friendly initiatives from your own home. Growing and tending to your own personal homestead can be hard work, but it's worth it for the satisfaction and security of being able to provide for yourself. By the time you have finished reading this book, you'll be a theoretical expert, ready to put this knowledge to work and start your backyard homestead!

7

CHAPTER 1
PREPARE YOURSELF

COMMITMENT IS KEY

The hardest part about starting your own homestead or really any project is committing to it. Starting the job is half the work. Preparing yourself to face any task you may take on is just as important as the work you put into the task itself. When it comes to sustainable living, it is especially important to prepare yourself for the road ahead. Unfortunately, we live in a very fast-paced society and changing your lifestyle to be more environmentally conscious can take a lot of effort. You can do it, though, and once you understand all of the elements that go into creating a successful homestead, you'll be growing your own food in no time.

Commitment is the first and most important step in starting any project, especially one as important as your new homestead. It's one thing to say you will start and do the research, but it is another thing entirely to follow through with all the hard work that comes next. We've all had goals that we set and then gave up on, and that's okay. For this homestead, though, you want to make a promise, a commitment to yourself and your future, that you will work hard and make it to the extraordinary payoff.

The key to commitment and follow-through is setting goals. Set big, overarching, long-term goals to look forward to, and smaller, step-by-step goals that you can achieve with some dedicated work. Setting a straightforward and definite goal for yourself will help you to visualize the outcome of all your hard work. If you start your homestead just thinking about all the different possibilities, you will be stuck daydreaming forever. Try focusing on one specific aspect of the homestead that you really want to see come to fruition. When challenges arise that you must overcome, go back to your main goal and remember what you are working towards. If you can picture the outcome in your head, you can make it a reality!

Almost as important as commitment is focus. Without focus and direction, your goals will be just that: goals. In order to achieve your backyard homestead, you are going to have to work hard and stay on task. Many people tend to struggle with big projects because they get easily distracted, and once you get distracted, it can be hard to return to work. Obstacles and challenges may arise, and there will be roadblocks that you will need to overcome. Without focus, you will get lost in these distractions and find yourself stuck with a half-finished garden instead of a flourishing homestead. When challenges do arise, an emotional response can also cloud your judgment, and it may become difficult to see your next steps. Staying focused can help you remember your purpose and the goal you're working towards. Throughout this journey you are embarking on, always remember to go back to the original reasons you decided to start your own homestead and focus on your main goals.

Through focus, commitment, and determination, you can achieve any goal, whether your backyard homestead is a small garden or a vast farm. When it comes to your goals, set large, overarching ones, and plan them out in detail before you begin. When you're in the middle of working, the little things can distract you or stop you in your tracks if you let them. As we've already mentioned, a backyard homestead will require hard work, meaning it will be tough at times. It's important to not let little setbacks get you too riled up, because with the right efforts, the final product will be so worth it. Always keep moving forward, take on one problem at a time, and keep going, even if you feel like quitting. Sustainable living is achievable, and once you get through the initial difficulties of focus and commitment, you'll be making massive progress in no time!

BENEFITS OF HOMESTEADING

Why should you start a homestead? The list of benefits is absolutely infinite! There are so many amazing reasons to start your very own homestead. You can grow your own food, raise your own animals, live a more sustainable life, not have to rely as much on outside factors for your resources, and so much more! Homesteading is hard work, but it can be so rewarding when done properly. Especially living in today's fast-paced world of political and economic turmoil, having your own source of resources can be crucial to maintaining your own personal health and happiness. Moreover, the time is now for each of us to start doing our part to heal this earth and help prevent environmental damage that add to the effects of climate change. There are innumerable great reasons to start your own backyard homestead, so in order to prepare you, we want to discuss just a few now to get you motivated and ready to work!

If nothing else, homesteading can provide you with important resources such as food and other plant or animal by-products. It will also teach you the importance of hard work and build your strength physically and emotionally. Working on a homestead, having to tend to the land and raise plants and animals will build such a strong work ethic. It is a big responsibility and commitment, and to make the decision to start your own homestead will teach you so many important life lessons. By growing your own food and creating energy and sustenance for yourself completely from scratch, your outlook on life will be drastically changed and make you a stronger and more well-rounded human being.

Homesteading will also greatly humble you. It can be a difficult process at times, and mistakes show. Forget to water one of your plants on time? The whole thing may die, meaning you have to start again. Crops can die, structures can fall over, etc. Whether it be by accident or mistake, life happens, and homesteading can be frustrating. It's the challenges that make it so rewarding, though, and overcoming these mistakes or obstacles you may face will keep you humble, build your endurance, and make you a better homesteader and per son. Keep up your perseverance, focus on your goals, and improve every day; that's how you learn any new skill, and that is what makes life all the more worth living. The sweet reward of successfully cultivating your crops or taking care of your animals will be all the sweeter after you've faced the hardships of the work.

Homesteading also tastes so much better. If you're a foodie or have a very distinguished palate—you can always tell the difference between fresh, locally-grown fruits and vegetables, and the long-haul, prefrozen, store-bought whatever. The same goes for meat from animals. You can taste the difference between naturally-raised, grass-fed chickens vs the stuff you get from factory farming that's pumped full of chemicals and hormones. Food grown organically and locally always tastes 100 times better, and you can be certain that it was grown or raised with love and care. Even if you aren't the kind of person who can normally taste the difference, just knowing that your own hard work and effort went into creating and preparing the food you eat will make it taste far better.

Homegrown food always tastes the best. Besides, homesteading will also boost your appreciation of the foods you eat. Knowing how much hard work you put into making sure your food grows full and delicious will only increase your pride and your joy of getting to eat. Knowing all the effort you put into planting, tending to, and harvesting your crops makes the reward of feasting on it even better than before.

This remains all the more true when it comes to meat. Raising animals for their meat is a difficult process that takes an incredible amount of work and willpower. Raising animals is a lot different than tending to crops and takes even more responsibility and perseverance. When you buy meat from the butcher or the grocery store, you don't have to think about all the hard work that goes into raising an animal. You think even less about the difficulty it takes to then kill and butcher the animal and prepare the meat for consumption. It takes not only a lot of effort and physical strength, but intense emotional strength and resilience as well. Being the one to raise, kill, and prepare the meat yourself can teach you the true value of what you consume, and it will show you how to be more conscious of what you eat and when.

Homesteading is also such a great teacher of all kinds of life lessons. Obviously, you will learn how to tend to your crops, raise your animals, keep everything running smoothly, etc. But there is so much more you learn. Hard work teaches you perseverance, as we've mentioned; it teaches you about where life comes from, and how precious it is. Tending to your own food teaches you the value of every part of the system; without water or sunlight, your plants won't grow, and without your own input, it can all fall apart. Homesteading will teach you about the earth and its needs, as well as your own needs and your families' needs. You can learn how to prepare your food and cook it more efficiently or in different, delicious ways. The patterns and life cycles of honey bees, turning milk to cheese, water and energy usage, how to gut a chicken, how to perform first aid, etc. All of these things and more can be learned through homesteading and commitment to the craft.

THE HOMESTEADING MINDSET

Before you can begin working on your homestead, you need to first change your mind, or rather, your mindset. In order to live a viable, environmentally-friendly lifestyle, you need to shift your perspective away from consumerism and towards sustainability. This means focusing more on how you can make, remake, or reuse the tools and materials you have at your disposal instead of buying things you may not need. The goal of homesteading is to be self-sufficient and not need to rely on consumerism or capitalism to get you through your day. The first step to living a happier, more peaceful life and becoming more in tune with the earth is to stop thinking about what you need and start thinking about what you already have.

The first step to changing the way you think is to redefine your standards of success. Think about what success looks like to you. If success means making a lot of money, buying expensive clothes and a fancy car, then you have a long road ahead of you. The main goals of your homestead should be security, sustainability, and self-reliance. Once you are able to see these key elements as the standard of success, that's when the real change will begin. Success doesn't even need to be measured by productivity, but simply by the effort you are making. If you are working hard, and you can recognize that you are doing your best, then each day will be a successful one on your homestead.

Changing your views of success can be a difficult thing to learn, or rather, unlearn. Everything we view as successful in modern society is held by the standards of capitalism, meaning that success directly relates to money. As we said before, your homestead is about self-reliance, harnessing your value as an individual, putting your energy into making yourself a better person, and making the world a better place. Once your focus is on the work instead of the possible outcomes, that is when you will be able to start your best work.

Another important tip to remember when working on your own personal homestead is to always be prepared to adapt your plan. Sometimes things won't go your way, whether it be by accident, mistake, or just sheer bad luck. You should always keep in mind that Mother Nature is a fickle lady, and her mood will affect your plans. Being able to improve, shift, or adapt your plans into something new when things don't go the way you want is crucial in the homesteading world.

Maybe your chickens aren't laying enough eggs or your crops aren't doing too well. Your plans will have to change along with the whims of the planet, and maybe you'll have to start raising ducks instead of chickens or plant different crops for the season. Nothing ever needs to be set in stone, and you should always be open to learning new things.

For many people, even just starting a homestead is a brand new area of knowledge, and learning something completely new can be hard, but don't be intimidated. Homesteading techniques and tricks change every season, and people are always coming up with new, better ways to work. Even professionals can learn something new every day. Always be open to trying new things and learning new techniques or habits for your homestead. Instead of facing your failure at something and feeling defeated, focus on ways in which you can overcome your obstacles, even if it's as simple as how you can improve next time around. Learning new ways to find success on your homestead is the most important part of long-term prosperity for you and your homestead.

As we've mentioned, your mindset means everything when it comes to your homestead.

Remaining positive in the face of adversity, staying focused on your goals, and using your struggles as fuel to your pursuits is the only way to stay on track and find success. Every obstacle you face in your homestead can be overcome; if not this season, then in the next. Finally, make sure you are open and excited to change. Change will come regardless of the plans you make and the hard work you put in, so always be prepared to change your mindset and your plans to overcome whatever challenges it may bring. Homesteaders must be resilient as well as adaptable, so don't be afraid to embrace the adversity fully, so that both you and your homestead come out the other side stronger.

YOUR FIRST GOALS

The very first part of building your homestead is to set your goals. Obviously, these goals may shift, change, or even grow once you get to work, but setting the initial goals will propel you into the homesteading lifestyle. These first goals should include your budgets, target dates, what crops you will be growing or animals you will be raising, and more. The purpose of these first goals is to give you a good baseline for your homestead planning. Your budget and target dates will determine what you grow and when, as well as give you an idea of what structures or equipment you may need to build or acquire beforehand. While the plan may change as you go, these first goals that you set will be the backbone of your entire homestead, so we want to make sure you are ready and informed for anything and everything!

Sometimes, the process of just setting a goal can be over whelming, especially when you are just starting. Having a clear, set goal is the first step to any plan, though, and completely necessary for any successful project, particularly something as important as a homestead. A properly written goal can guide you through the entire process from start to finish and gives you a determined target for which to aim. A well-planned goal should follow the 'SMART' method. That is, it should be Specific, Measurable, Achievable, Relevant, and Time-bound (Carleo, 2017). Using these criteria, you can ensure that your goals are well-thought-out and prioritize your success.

When you follow the SMART system of setting a goal, you can easily see the steps to your plan unfolding even before you begin. A goal must be 'Specific' enough that success or failure can be easily determined. Your goal should also be 'Measurable'; when it comes to homesteading, your success will be measured in land, yield, time, energy, and even profit. Your goal should take all of these measurements into account. Next up is 'Achievable', which is pretty self-explanatory. Your goal should be realistic in respect to what you have at your disposal and your own capabilities. Next is 'Relevance', and in terms of homesteading, this step is pretty simple. Make sure your goal is relevant to the work you are doing on your homestead, and make sure that the goal makes sense to follow through in the time and space with which you will be working. Finally, we reach 'Time-bound', which means that you need to set a deadline. A goal without a deadline is just procrastination. Making a deadline will encourage you to work hard and helps you to hold yourself accountable for your own success or failure.

To set a proper goal, you must first determine two things: where you are trying to go and when you want to arrive. Knowing where you start off and where you are aiming to helps create a timeline and a loose plan for how you will work to achieve your goal. Be specific, and set different goals for each individual aspect of your homestead. The more specificity in your goals, the easier you will find it to follow through. For beginner homesteaders, your first goal should be to learn and prepare yourself and your land. Reading this book is already a great first step to take towards achieving that goal!

BUDGETING FOR YOUR HOMESTEAD

One extremely important thing to keep in mind when planning your homestead is your budget. Especially when you are just getting started, budgeting is an essential part of the homesteading process. Luckily, budgeting for any project always follows similar patterns, so if you've ever had to budget for a big project before now, you already know most of what you will need. Homesteading, like any other project, requires careful planning in regards to spendings, earnings, and budgets. The first stages of building your homestead will require purchasing or building equipment, starters, planters, soil, and much more. Knowing the cost and value of everything you're going to need is crucial as you begin your journey of homestead-living.

The most important part of any good budget is to write it down. Whether it be on paper, online, in an app, or whatever you may choose, get those numbers out of your head and into the physical world. Your mind isn't foolproof, and you will forget things, so keeping track of everything is crucial. The second most important part of a budget is research. No matter what you are buying or saving for, always do your research first. When it comes to homesteading, maybe you're thinking of raising chickens, in which case you're going to need a coop, feed, and much more. Do your research into the cost of every element you need to purchase, and keep track of all your expenses so you know how much you've put into a project.

When it comes to expenses and budgeting, all projects come with the same tips and tricks to keep you on top of your money. Always know the difference between your wants and needs, and do your research before buying anything import ant. When it comes to larger purchases, maybe you want to get a tractor to make taking care of your homestead easier; always sleep on it! Waking up in the morning with a clear mind gives you new insight into most aspects of life, especially budgeting for the homestead.

RULES AND REGULATIONS

One important piece of research you need to do before starting your homestead is finding out about the homesteading laws and regulations in your area. Always check the laws for your region or municipality before doing any construction or land preparation. You don't want to get caught off guard by a surprise visit from a bylaw officer. Knowing the rules surrounding homesteads and farms for your region is crucial to the preparation process.

In the United States, there is what's called a "Homestead Exemption" that is applicable in many states. The "Homestead Exemption" is a legal act that protects homesteaders and has a few different benefits. In most states, you must submit an application in order to qualify for this exemption, so be sure to do your research regardless of where you live. The benefits of this Homestead Exemption relate to property taxes and tax loss reimbursement. Check out more information on your government website for the Homestead Exemption opportunities in your area.

PREPPING YOUR HOME

Finally, the last step of the planning process is to prepare your home. Homesteading takes up space, so make sure you clear out anything you don't need around your property that may just be taking up space. You are going to need to be capable of fending for yourself on your homestead, so make sure that the entire area is properly cleaned and ready to go. Whatever space you have, whether it's a large plot of farmland or a small suburban backyard, make sure you clear out as much of the area as possible before you begin. Then, you're going to want to build or set up some sheds.

BUILDING A SHED

Regardless of what kinds of crops you want to grow or animals you want to raise, you are going to need shed space. Whether it be for storing equipment, soil, seeds, extra materials, or any other number of things that may be useful on your homestead, you are going to need a shed or two in your yard to keep it all organized. Not to worry though; building a shed is pretty simple, and if the task seems a little daunting, there are always options for purchasing one and having it installed or even getting a kit with all the components and putting it together yourself.

A simple shed is pretty easy to construct, seeing as it is basically just a large box with a roof and a door. We've already discussed the budget and bylaw aspects you need to consider before building a shed, but you should also consider the weather in your area and the properties of the ground on which you will be building. If you live in a hilly area, or have a sloping yard where you plan on setting up your homestead, you may need to take some extra steps in building your shed.

The foundation of any building is the first and most important step, so make sure you have a strong foundation that's properly measured before you continue building. If this is your first building project, we recommend closely following a guide from a credible source or enlisting the help of someone who has worked on similar projects previously. If this isn't an option, your local hardware store will likely have all the tools and equipment you need to get started. Don't be afraid to ask the hardware store employees for their advice or help, either, especially when you are a beginner. There are also a number of DIY guides and videos online that detail exactly how to build a shed, ranging from a tiny gardening box to a whole barn house, so don't be afraid to watch some tutorials or read a few blogs!

After the foundation, the roof is the most important part of any building. It must be sturdy and strong, but not too heavy so as to put weight on the walls and support structures. Depending on what you use to construct your shed, you may need to use specific roofing materials. Your local hardware store should be able to advise you on this as well, but we would recommend using felt, bitumen roof sheets, bitumen shingles, plastic lightweight roof tiles, or wood shingles to create a sturdy and waterproof roofing to your shed.

POWERING YOUR HOMESTEAD

When it comes to power, there are a few different options you may want to investigate before you begin your homestead. Some smaller equipment you'll be working with is battery-powered or electric, and that's fine for the small stuff. You may find, however, that your homestead requires a lot more power than you can justify adding to your electric bill. In that case, you may want to look into solar power options or even erecting a windmill for power storage. This may seem difficult or too far out of your comfort zone, but not to worry; we've got you covered!

Solar power is actually quite simple. Solar panels are made up of silicon. Photovoltaic cells capture sunlight and convert it into electricity. The electricity can then be used to power just about anything in and around your home. Solar panels can be easily installed onto your rooftop or even the roof of a shed. The panels will generate direct current electricity, which must be fed into an inverter to then become alternating current electricity. Then, with the use of a switchboard, you will be able to utilize this electricity wherever you may need it. Any unused electricity that your solar panels provide will get fed directly into your city's electricity grid, which also earns you credit towards your electricity bills.

Solar panels can be extremely useful, especially when working on a homestead. After installation, they require little maintenance and provide quality power for a long time. The only components are the solar panels, the inverter, a switch board, and a mandatory utility meter that your electric company can install for you. Afterward, you will have power from the sun running all your tools and equipment. If it seems a little complicated, you can always give your local solar power company a call and ask for a consultation. Solar power will help reduce the cost of electricity, provide for not only you but your entire neighborhood by feeding into the power grid, generate backup power for nighttime or outages, and operate efficiently on both small and large scales. It's even environ mentally conscious as it takes up very little space, and all the energy comes from a renewable resource. You can find out more in our book specifically catered towards off-grid solar power.

Another option when it comes to powering your homestead is wind turbines. Though they can be expensive to erect initially, wind turbines provide energy at a constant and consistent rate. Definitely do some research on wind turbines and whether this system will be right for you and your homestead. If you live in a residential or urban area, it is likely that you will run into too many conflicts with zoning regulations and local homeowner associations, but if you are in a rural area and have space, a windmill could be just what you need to complete your eco-friendly, home power system.

Even in less than optimal wind conditions, a turbine can easily provide enough power to boost your system. Renewable energy experts often recommend a combination of solar and wind power systems for people looking to live more sustainably or even off-grid.

LIFE ON THE HOMESTEAD

Now that you're informed, it's time to start working towards building and running your homestead. It will be difficult at first, especially if you are used to living a comfy life. Homesteading requires effort, determination, commitment, and perseverance. It's completely 100 percent worth it, though, and while it may be a lot of work, there are so many reasons to get started on your homestead today.

Homesteading will provide you with a better connection to nature and to your food. When you grow and raise your own food, you know its entire life cycle, from start to finish. You also know exactly what goes into making the food you eat, so you never again have to worry about added sugars or salts or even chemical additives that are used in processed foods. Going organic tastes so much better and knowing that it was your own hard work that went into making something will make it all the more delicious.

Homesteading will also provide you with freedom and security. You are no longer going to need to rely on corporations and big chain grocery stores to provide you with healthy, organic options. By working on your homestead, you will be able to provide yourself and your community with delicious, natural foods for a much better price. You will also have the ability to store and save everything you grow. Homesteading provides you with all the food you could need should you encounter hard times.

Homesteading will change your life forever. Get ready to become a happier, healthier, stronger, smarter, and more rounded version of yourself. It's hard work, but anything worth it always is. Once you start working on your homestead, you will learn so many new things. Your palate will develop as you eat better, your fitness will improve as you work harder, and even your mood will be better once you start working on something that you know will benefit you and your family. Yes, homesteading will change your mindset and perspective of the world for the better, and it will make you a completely different person. That's a good thing, though! Your homestead will provide for you just as much work as you put into it.

CHAPTER 2
READY THE LAND

Now that you are mentally prepared, it's time to physically prepare for your homestead! Just like any big project, a homestead requires some physical preparation before you really begin. You need to clear the space, prep the land, and even figure out some logistics like plumbing and irrigation. You know by now that homesteading is no small task; it's going to take some work, but it'll pay off when you finally get to chow down on that fresh, homegrown produce.

You want your homestead to be as successful as possible, which means that preparation is key. By prepping the area in which you'll be working, you can guarantee that you are giving your crops or animals their best chance to not only survive, but thrive this season. Prepping your homestead means working on the land around you, building the structures you may need, such as fences or plant boxes, and even plumbing and outdoor wiring. All of these steps are recommended though not necessary, and depending on the size and scope of the land you're working with, you may have to tweak some things or skip some steps to make it work for you. That's totally fine! As long as you're working your hardest and using everything you've got, you'll do great!

TERRAFORMING YOUR HOMESTEAD

Before you can plant anything, you need to lay down some groundwork. Depending on where you live, you may not be able to successfully grow any plants without first using extra soil and fertilizer. That's alright, though, because soil is all around us, and making your own compost is easier than you might think!

Making your own compost is super easy, and it can take your garden game to the next level. Now, the best compost is made with an equal mix of greens and browns. Greens are nitrogen-filled materials like manure, green grass, or weeds. The brown materials, like straw, dried leaves, or wood chips, are all high in carbon. With this winning combination of nitrogen and carbon, you can kick-start your at-home compost system that recycles and reuses any organic material you don't need. The benefits, aside from being environmentally-friendly, are that your compost can be used to fertilize your crops and help them grow bigger, better, and stronger.

Another great trick for your homestead, especially if you don't have much space, is to try dry gardening. Instead of having your crops all spread out, grow them densely together, and plant the roots as deep as you can to encourage stronger growth. From there, water minimally. Though plants need lots of water to thrive, growing them slowly by watering less—or using a drip irrigation system—can make them stronger and more resilient and increase your chances of having them grow back even stronger next season. Dry gardening is especially useful if you live in a more arid climate or to prepare in case of an emergency like a water shortage or a drought. Garlic and potatoes are a couple of great candidates for dry gardening, as they can easily grow closely together and excess water can actually dilute their taste, which you don't want.

If you are going to raise animals, it's extremely beneficial to grow food for them as well. Instead of buying feed, save money and time by planting foods that your animals can chow down on as well.

Chickens can eat all kinds of different seeds, such as pumpkin and sunflower, as well as corn, cooked or raw root vegetables, and most of your kitchen scraps. Horses can eat grass from almost anywhere, certain kinds of nontoxic weeds, and even veggies right from your kitchen. Cows and goats are similar and can even eat alfalfa and the leaves off of raspberry plants. Feeding your animals with homegrown food is not only healthier for them as it is all-natural, but it also helps with your homestead maintenance. The animals can eat a lot of the 'leftovers' of the food you grow that aren't appropriate or appetizing for humans. If you are going to raise animals, we definitely recommend acquiring a hand scythe to cut grass for feed and growing winter squash, a delicious option that is good for almost all farm animals.

When it comes time to finally plant and grow your crops, aim for a flat and sunny spot. Most homestead crops require a lot of direct sunlight, but this can vary depending on what you are growing and where you live. Crops will also grow best on flat terrain, as sloped or hilly areas can be more susceptible to change and deterioration under harsh weather conditions. Planting something on a hill can also mess with the roots, which ideally grow downwards and outwards. On a sloped surface, the roots may grow at odd angles, affecting the growth of the entire plant.

GARDEN STRUCTURES

There are a few different structures you will almost certainly need to build or buy when starting your homestead. Planter boxes, raised beds, soil blocks, and possibly even some grow lights, are all necessary for the healthy and hearty growth of tons of different plants. Not to worry; all the supplies you need can be easily acquired from a hardware store or garden center, and many of these projects are pretty simple.

Raised beds and planter boxes are the easiest garden structures to build yourself, but you can always buy premade ones from your local garden center. All you need is some planks of wood, some 2x4s, screws, and a drill. Obviously, the sizing is going to depend on how big you want your planter boxes to be, how much space you have/need, and how high off the ground you want your raised beds to be. For these kinds of projects, you can easily get the materials you need and then do the measurements and cuts at home with a circular saw. If you aren't comfortable cutting the wood yourself just yet, do not worry; your local hardware store should be able to do it for you if you request.

The main thing to worry about with planter boxes is proper measurements. You want to ensure that your plants have the best chance to grow and thrive, and that means making sure that their home is in the ideal conditions. Measure twice and cut once, as the saying goes. You don't want to accidentally make one side longer than the other and have your whole garden suddenly growing lopsided.

Another especially helpful tip We've learned from our own gardening experience is to layer your planter boxes—especially ones that are raised above ground—with plastic lining and garden fabric before adding soil. Not only does the layering take some of the pressure off the box once you add the soil, but it also helps preserve your planter boxes from water damage when you are watering and tending to your plants. You can easily cut and place a sheet of plastic lining and staple it into place or use screws over the plastic to keep it in place. Don't forget to cut the drainage hole in the bottom of your planter boxes and the plastic lining if you choose to add it. Without proper drainage, your plants may get overwatered, or the weight of the wet soil will put extra, unnecessary pressure on the planter boxes.

Before you can plant anything in your garden beds, though, you need to grow your seedlings indoors. Growing your seed lings under a glow lamp or even just near a window in your house before planting them outside can really make-or-break your season. Many types of seeds will not grow under harsh conditions, and if you plant them in the ground too early in the year, they will die before they even start to sprout. Using a grow light to grow your seedlings before planting them can promote stronger growth after they are transferred and give them a better chance of surviving and growing strong. Grow your seedlings in small containers or napkins with nutrient-dense soil in greenhouse-like conditions; meaning lots of sun and water. If you don't have a good spot in your house that gets lots of natural sunlight, you can purchase a grow light to help with this.

A great tool that we recommend for beginner homesteaders is a "soil blocker". It is a small tool that takes loose soil and com presses it into tight blocks, just like those that you would get in a seedling tray, only without the excess plastic components. Not only is this method extremely easy and more sustainable as it uses less plastic, but it's actually far more practical than some other methods as well. For instance, using plastic seedling trays can often take up a lot of unnecessary space. These trays are also not optimal for root growth, as the plants grow at different rates and some will outgrow the tray before others have even sprouted. Furthermore, depending on the scope of your homestead, you may not need a full tray of certain seedlings, meaning that half a tray is just empty and taking up space. With the soil block method, you can make as many soil blocks as you need, and they are much easier to transfer into your garden when the time comes.

Another project you may want to include in your homestead is an arbor or trellis. These are beautiful decorative pieces but can also be extremely useful if you are growing vines or other plants that may need a structure to help them stay upright when they grow. Beans, peas, cucumbers, and even summer squash and some types of melons need a trellis or ladder structure to help them remain upright while they grow to fruition. The type of trellis you need will vary depending on what you are growing, but a basic trellis can be made with a couple of wooden posts and some twine. For something a little sturdier, try using chicken wire and attaching that to the wooden posts instead. If you want to go a bit fancier, there are many arbor and trellis options that you can purchase online or at a garden center, or you could build your own by following one of the many DIY's available for free online.

FENCES

The next structures you're going to need on your homestead are some fences. This will be particularly useful when it comes to raising animals, as you will need to learn how to build and repair the animal pens. We'll talk about raising animals a little later in Chapter 5, but for now, let's focus on getting these fences set up. Whether it be a picket fence to surround your garden or a sturdy gate to keep wild animals off your land, strong fences are essential for any homestead.

The first step to building a fence is to set up the fence posts. If you don't set the posts up properly, the efficacy of the en tire structure will be compromised. When putting up a fence post, you first want to dig a hole in the dirt where you'll be placing it about 12 to 18 inches deep. You can choose to go shallower or deeper, but this is the depth we recommend to ensure a sturdy and robust post. The reason you need to dig so deep is that you are going to want to fill the hole with cement when you put the post in the ground. This is to create a strong foundation for the entire fence. You can also choose to add a couple of inches of peat gravel at the bottom of the hole before you put it in the cement and fence post. This will block the wooden post from resting directly against the earth and therefore protect it from any deterioration. Dirt and soil can easily rot wood after prolonged exposure, especially in moist conditions like that of a garden or homestead, so this step is vital to the durability of your fences.

When you first set up your fence post, be sure to check that it is level before anything else. Double-check after you've added the cement mix, and then triple-check it after the cement has had time to harden and solidify. Once you are absolutely certain that your fence post is upright and sturdy, that's when you should proceed with the rest of the fence. The type of fence you are building will dictate your next move. You may want to add metal braces if you are looking to build a larger, stronger fence. For something small and simple, though, you can easily just connect the horizontal planks directly to your fence post. This is also a great way to make a homemade trellis or arbor; just add a cross beam at the top and bottom of your fence posts and add twine, string, chicken wire, or whatever other material you may be using.

One way to easily set up a long fence is called 'stretching'. This method is especially useful for large field fences that are very long and would take a lot of time to set up each individual section. It works by rolling out wire fencing along a long, straight stretch of fence posts and then putting it all up at once. What you need for this method is your already installed fence posts and a large roll of chicken wire or another wire fencing. First, attach one section of wire fencing to your initial two fence posts. This must be done after you've put in your 2x4s—or whatever wood you may be using—for structural support. You can use a staple gun to keep the wire fencing connected and then add nails as you see fit for structural integrity.

Now, using the rest of your roll of wire fencing, lay it on the ground, and unroll it along the straight length of all your fence posts. The wiring should only be attached to the very first two fence posts and line up on the ground next to the rest of the fence line from there. Make sure it is in a straight line, flat on the ground, and even. Once that is done, you are going to use a metal 'T'-post and weave it through the wire fencing at the end of your straightaway. This is going to be your come along; the part that holds everything together. It should also be placed only a few feet past the final fence post. From here, you are going to attach the 'T'-post to the bumper of a truck, car, tractor, or any other strong motorized vehicle using some metal chains. Then, very carefully and gently, use the vehicle to pull the entire length of the wire fencing up against your fence posts. If done correctly, the wire fencing should stand up vertically and pull against the fence posts due to the ten sion from the first fence post being pulled by the vehicle. Make sure you go slow and steady so as not to break anything or move it out of place. Keeping the line taut, make sure your vehicle is turned off and head back out to your fence. The wire fencing should all be upright against your fence posts now, minus the last one, which was attached to the vehicle.

You can now go back along your fence line and attach the wire fencing to all of the posts using staples, nails, wire-wrapping techniques, or whatever other method you may find works best. If you are using metal fence posts throughout the length of your fence line, we recommend getting little wire fence clips that attach on either side of the metal post and keep the wire fencing upright and connected to the fence post. All you need to apply these clips is a pair of pliers to wrap them tightly around the wire fencing for security. Once your wire fencing is fully connected to each fence post, you can head back to your vehicle, reverse slightly to slacken the chains, and release the tension, and then remove the chains from your come along post. From here, you can remove or leave the come along post to your liking, as long as the last fence post in the row, prior to the come-along piece, is a sturdy wooden post with a crossbeam for support. If you have more long stretches of fencing (for example, if you are enclosing a large field for horses or cows), repeat these steps on each straightaway you have in your fence. Now your wire fence is complete!

To build a picket fence is a little different because it is a much smaller structure. You will still need to use a similar method of putting up the initial fence posts, including digging a deep hole and adding cement to keep it locked in place for a long time. Place your fence posts no more than eight feet apart, otherwise your 2x4s won't fit properly. Just like how you would for a regular fence, you are going to want to attach a metal brace to hold your 2x4s properly. For the best results and the sturdiest fence, you should have one 2x4 near the top of the fence posts and one near the bottom. This will ensure that your fence is properly supported once you start adding the pickets. Once your fence posts are all connected, it's time to get started on the pickets. You can purchase specific wood for picket fences at a hardware store or make your own using 1x6 fence boards and cutting them to your desired length. Cutting these boards yourself will take some extra time, but can also save you some money. Don't forget to cut off the top of the boards at a 45-degree angle on either side to make a nice, pointed tip to your picket fence.

When it comes time to attach the pickets to your fence, it can be a little tricky to get the spacing right without a proper guide. Using one of your pickets, you can make a guide by attaching a spare block of wood to the top right above the level at which the upper 2x4 is attached. Then attach another, slightly longer block of wood to create a sort of hook that can be easily placed over the upper 2x4 of the fence and pushed along the length of the 2x4. By doing this, you effectively create a spacing guide for your picket fence. Screw on the first picket, then use your guide by placing it right up next to the newly installed picket. Attach your second picket on the other side of the guide you built, and when you remove the guide, the two pickets will be perfectly spaced. Repeat this process across the rest of your fence as you continue to add the pickets to ensure that they are all evenly-spaced. The spacer guide that you've created will ensure that everything is evenly-spaced and uniform across the entire fence. Now that your fence is built, all that's left is to paint it whatever bright and vibrant color you want!

Now, you can always hire someone to come in and help install a fence for you. However, installation is generally charged per foot of fencing, which can get pretty pricey. Building your own fence is always going to be the cheaper alternative.

Especially if you are planning on raising animals and are going to need multiple fences of different sizes and styles, it is always better to do it yourself if you feel confident. There are so many free resources and guides available online to help you if you get lost along the way, and the rewarding feeling of completing a project on your own will be so worth it. Plus, all the money you will save on installation fees won't hurt, either.

Depending on where you live, you may want to consider a solar-powered electric fence. An electric fence can be extremely beneficial at protecting your animals and crops from local predators, such as coyotes, wolves, or even bears. If you have space and live in a region where these animals are common, you may want to consider it, and using solar power to run your electric fence will keep you off-grid and eco friendly. An electric fence provides a low-damage shock to any animals, domestic or wild, that touch it. This keeps wild animals out and your own domestic and/or farm animals in. An electric fence often needs a power source, however, and having outlets in the great outdoors is not really an option. That's why solar power is the best way to go and has so many more benefits. The cost of installing an AC power unit, especially if you live in a rural area, and installing one yourself can be dangerous if you don't know what you are doing. Using a solar power charger to power your fence instead is much simpler and can save you a ton of money. Solar power saves you money on electrical bills and can keep your homestead running in the event of a storm or power outage using the stored backup energy it has saved after many days of sun exposure.

GATES

The most important part of a fence is a good, strong gate. If you make your fence all the way around in a perfect square, how are you going to get in and water your crops or feed your animals? Whenever you build your fence, remember to leave an open space at some point to insert a gate; otherwise, you are going to have to do some intense climbing or jumping every time you want to get inside! Building a gate for your fences is easy once you've put up the entire fence because it is the equivalent of one small section and is basically just a fence on hinges.

To build a gate, you are going to need almost all the same materials you used to build your fence, plus some metal hinges and a gate lock or handle of some sort to use when you want to open and close it. Once again, you can always purchase a gate and install it, or you can build one yourself. Building it yourself is always going to be cheaper, though more time-consuming, so it's up to you to decide what's worth it for your situation.

The most important thing about building your own gate is to make sure it is structurally sound. This means that you are go ing to want to double-layer it in a way, basically sandwiching your support beams between two 2x4s on either side. To start your homemade gate, cut four pieces of wood—we recommend 2x4s—to the desired length that will be the height of your gate. Remember that this does not mean the same height as your fence, as the gate is going to be off the ground and also may not need to be the full height of your fence, depending on what it will be used for in the end. You will also need to cut three pieces of wood to your desired gate length and a final diagonal piece that will be used for structural support. This last piece can be cut out after you've constructed the gate so that you can double-check the length.

When you put the gate together, place the three crossbeams you cut down on top of two of the side beams, creating two equal windows of space. These three crossbeams are your upper, middle, and lower support pieces to your gate. Once you've screwed them together, measure out and cut a square of wire fencing to attach. Make sure you attach the wire fencing directly to the three crossbeams, which will be on the inside of the gate. After that, place the last two wood planks over top of the rest of the gate, attaching them to the original two planks that mark the length of the gate. This will sandwich in your crossbeams and wire fencing, ensuring that they won't slip or easily come apart. This step is crucial in making sure your gate will be sturdy and long-lasting. Finally, mea sure the length from one corner of your gate to the opposite corner, and cut a final plank of wood to that length. Make sure that you cut the ends at a 45 degree angle so that they fit to the gate properly.

Now that your gate is fully built, you need to attach the hinges. Depending on how large your gate is, you may need to buy larger or smaller hinges in order to hold up the weight of the gate. When attaching the hinges, you most likely only need two: one at the top and one at the bottom. However, if your gate is larger and heavier, three may be necessary to ensure structural integrity. Once the hinges are on, get someone to help you hold your gate in place while you make a mark on your fence post one inch below the spot where each hinge will connect. Then, you are going to attach the other piece of the hinge to your fence post and attach the gate. Make sure that when you attach the gate to the fence post, you are attaching so that the diagonal beam across your gate is at the bottom corner where the hinge will connect. You want the diagonal beam to be leaning towards the opening of the gate as it will help keep the gate robust and sturdy for longer. After that, all that's left is to screw on whatever handle or opening mechanism you are using to the other side of the gate. Again, make sure the handle is in the same upper corner as the diagonal cross plank to ensure maximum structural integrity.

PLUMBING AND WIRING

The last part of your homestead you're going to need to set up is outdoor plumbing and wiring. It is crucial to your homestead's success that you have a good irrigation system for your crops and a properly built and well-functioning electrical circuit for anything you may need to use electricity for while you work. We are going to cover the basics for outdoor plumbing and electrical wiring; however, you may need a little less, a little more, or a little different depending on your homestead. Remember, whatever works best for you is best for your homestead!

LOW-TECH PLUMBING

Now, low-tech plumbing isn't for everyone, but if you are looking to save money on your water bill while maintaining a full homestead in need of crop irrigation and water for animals, you may want to try it out. One of the easiest ways to acquire water for your homestead is rain-catching. Especially if you live in a region with a rainy climate, collecting rainwater and using it for irrigation is a simple and easy way to save money and time. Obviously, when it rains you won't need to water your crops, but you can save extra water in rain catchers and store it in barrels or bins until you need it. This method can also be used to obtain drinking water for yourself and your animals; although, you have to be sure to purify the water before you consume it. You can do this by getting a water purifier, a purifying solution that can be added to rainwater to cleanse it, or go the good old-fashioned route and boil rainwater before consumption. Purifying the water before you drink it is extremely important, as water from anywhere can be contaminated with all kinds of germs and pathogens of which we may be unaware.

Another method for obtaining water is to tap a natural spring or underground aquifer. Tapping a nearby spring or stream is simple enough to do with a hose and spigot. Underground water is a little more complicated and will likely require some sort of well or piping. This is extremely difficult to do yourself, so we don't recommend it unless you have a professional on hand to assist. However, if you live on an old homestead that you are fixing up, you may want to scout around the property as there is likely already an old well that can be restored. If you live nearby a lake or river, you can also try to tap those in a similar fashion to a small stream. However, it may be more difficult as you must factor in currents and waves, as well as marine life. Regardless of where you are getting your water, make sure you are purifying and desalinating, if necessary. While it may not be bad for crops to drink up natural water from anywhere, you and your animals have a more complex digestive system, and dirty water can be a serious danger.

OUTDOOR WIRING

Outdoor wiring can be tricky, but it doesn't have to be difficult. Depending on what you need to power, you may not even need to do much work. First and foremost, check the regulations for your area to make sure that any permits you may require are in order before you start the project. Some places are very strict or specific about outdoor wiring or connecting your house's electrical supply to an outdoor shed. You are also going to want to figure out what works best for you: above-ground cables or underground wiring. Underground takes more work to set up, but is generally more stable and less likely to have any problems arise. That being said, if you do face electrical problems with underground cables, it is a lot harder to fix as you may have to dig the entire thing up again.

If you are going to need electricity for a lot of different things on your homestead, we recommend setting up an electrical shed where you can house any equipment or machinery that may be necessary. For example, you can set up a power inverter and storage unit, as well as a switchboard in a small shed to make optimal use of your outdoor electric system and protect the machinery from environmental elements. If you only need electricity for simple things like outdoor lighting, don't worry so much about needing an entire shed. For that, you may just want to run some cables out and set up some lights or lampposts in central areas.

Regardless of what you may be using outdoor electricity for, always consult a professional if you are unsure about something. Make sure you have all the necessary tools and supplies to complete your project before you begin. The last thing you want is to have loose cables or tools lying around while you run to the store to pick up something you forgot. That is an accident just waiting to happen. As with most of the projects we've already discussed, outdoor wiring is something you can hire a professional to do for you, although it is often a lot cheaper to do it yourself. That being said, electricity is not something you want to be messing around with if you haven't studied up on it first. Make sure you know exactly what your plan is and what safety measures to use before you start working.

To bury your wires underground and use the underground method of setting up your outdoor electric wiring, you are going to need an underground feeder cable. This is a specialized type of cable that you run the wiring through before burying what protects you from any possible damage to both the wires and the environment. Always check the regional guidelines or talk to an inspector about how deep your cables need to be run under the ground before you bury them. It is also important to have flexible conduits that you can easily insert or remove the wires from once buried. This will prevent you from needing to do any extra labor once the project is finished. You can use plastic tubing or PVC piping for this as it is sturdy and has adjustable joints that can be attached for proper direction. Always have an inspector or professional double-check your work before you bury your cable to ensure that it is done properly and safely. Once your wiring is all set up, you can connect it directly to whatever needs power, such as your lights, or you can connect it to a circuit board.

CHAPTER 3
GROWING CROPS THE

SUSTAINABLE WAY

The first step to running your sustainable homestead is to understand sustainable agriculture and how to grow crops responsibly, without harming the environment. The trick to a good homestead is to use everything you've got to the fullest extent. This means recycling old materials, repurposing junk to give it new life, and reducing your carbon footprint and environmental impact. The goal of sustainable agriculture—or in our case, sustainable homesteading—is to meet all of your present food and textile needs without harming the environment and the potential for the future. At every step of the process, there are ways we can be more environmentally conscious and make better decisions for the future of our planet.

Homesteading in itself is already a great way to live more sustainably, as you will not have to rely on corporations and industrial agriculture to fulfill your needs. You directly impact your patch of land by caring for it and tending to the plants and animals around you. You also indirectly impact so much more by running a homestead that you may not even realize. The more people who participate in homesteading and sustainable farming, the less need there will be for industrial agricultural practices that pollute the air and the earth in countless ways. Furthermore, any excess you may produce on your homestead can easily be given back to your community, whereas industrial agriculture is always producing in excess, leaving Mother Nature to take care of the dirty work.

One great way to ensure that you are farming sustainably is to grow the specific foods you may need. While you may be inclined to just go crazy and grow whatever you can, you should be wary of overproduction and overcrowding on your homestead. The human body is a complex system that requires many specific nutrients, vitamins, and minerals. Feed your body and keep your homestead neat by growing foods that are necessary for your health and wellness, without overproducing what you don't need. Growing foods such as squash, potatoes, broccoli, spinach, kale, and peppers is a good start as all of these delicious vegetables contain many of the necessary vitamins and minerals your body needs every day.

We've already discussed setting up a good compost system on your homestead, and this is just another great way to be a little more sustainable in your life. A good compost system can be fed pretty much any organic scraps and leftovers to create nutrient-rich fertilizer for your crops. One great composting tip is to introduce worms into your outdoor compost. Worms eat up organic materials and work to improve production of fertilizer for your homestead.

What to Grow on Your Homestead

At first, it can be difficult to decide what crops you should grow. Before you plant anything, make sure you are aware of the soil conditions and weather patterns in your area. A lot of crops require specific conditions in order to truly thrive on the home stead, so you don't want to start planting a bunch of randomly chosen seeds and do all the work to tend to them only to find out they won't grow due to environmental conditions that are out of your control. There are a lot of crops, however, that are extremely hearty and can grow in many different soil and weather conditions. These are going to be your essentials; the crops you absolutely need to have on your homestead. After you have the essentials, you can grow to your liking whatever else you may choose, but these crops are the ones we recommend.

ESSENTIAL CROPS

There are some crops that are just absolutely essential to have on your homestead. These fruits and vegetables are considered essential parts of any good garden, as they are hearty, nutrient-dense, and keep for a long time. These crops can save you in the event of a crisis and be delicious additions to your plate if not. They are easy to grow in a variety of different conditions, store well even without electricity or power, and are jam-packed with important nutrients to keep you strong and healthy.

The first is potatoes. The heartiest of foods, potatoes grow underground as root vegetables and are full of starchy, complex carbs that are healthy for you, and they can last a long time in storage. Potatoes actually produce more carbohydrates per square foot than any other vegetable that grows in the US. They are super easy to grow, can adapt to almost any soil conditions, and can withstand harsh weather conditions like rain or storms, unlike many other vegetables. They can also easily be stored without any power or electricity necessary for long periods of time. In some countries, potatoes are even grown without any irrigation.

Next up is corn, the most feasible of any grain product to grow successfully on a small homestead. It is rich in vitamins B_1, B_5, and C, contains minerals such as phosphorus and manganese, and also is dense in nutritional fiber. Grown in the summertime, this grain can also be easily stored during the cold months. It is perfect for hearty, starch-based sides such as corn bread or polenta, great for accompanying fresh meat from your homestead.

Beans, peas, and lentils are all super easy to grow and very nutritious. They are rich in protein and many other vitamins as well. Legumes are also quite easy to store without power or electricity, and different species of legumes can thrive in all sorts of different conditions. We recommend growing a variety of different types of beans and peas, and see what works best for you. You can grow several different species in a relatively small space as well.

Finally, squash. All kinds of squash are great, but winter squash specifically includes gourds such as pumpkins, but ternut squash, acorn squash, and many varieties of spaghetti squash. These delicious veggies are quite fruitful (pardon the pun), and though they take up a lot of garden space, the yield is almost equivalent. Winter squash is also much easier to store and keeps for much longer than their summer counterparts. You can display your gourds on your mantle or around the house until it's time to eat, and they will taste as good as ever.

These crops are your basic homestead essentials, but obviously, you can and should grow more if you have the space. Carrots, cabbage, spinach, onions, tomatoes, garlic, and as paragus are all great candidates for a successful homestead. Many of the crops are a lot easier to grow than you may think and can yield quite a bit, especially tomatoes and leafy greens such as lettuce and cabbages. Where you live can really affect the crops you are able to grow, so do some research before you plant anything. Finding out what type of plants will thrive in your region can save you a lot of work you would have otherwise put into growing a crop that may not even be able to survive the soil or weather conditions of your homestead.

BEST CROPS FOR YOUR HOMESTEAD

While all the essential crops we've gone over are some of the best things to grow, there are some that may be a bit more region-specific—or harder to grow—that are also very good to have on your homestead if you can swing it. The best crops are ones that are nutrient-dense, very hearty, store well, and most importantly: taste delicious!

We've already talked a little bit about corn, but to go into some more detail, you may want to try growing heirloom corn. Instead of just the sweet corn you may be used to, different varieties of heirloom corn can be useful for different situations. There are six types of corn altogether: sweet, popcorn, flint, flour, dent, and waxy. All of these have different conditions in which they thrive and different distinct properties that may be more or less suited to your homestead. Flint corn, for exam ple, grows in cooler, wetter climates, and flour corn is usually grown in the southwest, where it is hotter and dryer. Dent corn is the common field stuff that you are probably used to seeing. It is the easiest to grow and store, and the type we referred to ear lier in the chapter. Sweet corn is great to grow in the summer; a delicious addition to any barbeque. However, it doesn't store well and must be eaten or preserved after the initial harvest. It is up to you to decide which variety will work best for you, and this will depend on your environmental conditions as well as your personal preferences and your homesteads capabilities.

We've also already discussed potatoes and their many benefits, but we haven't yet talked about other root vegetables. Radishes, beets, carrots, and many more are all very hearty crops that are generally fast-growing due to their nature. Because these root vegetables grow underground, they often produce more than you'd expect and grow quite fast. Radishes are especially good as you can eat both the purple-red root and the leafy green top to this vegetable. Using the entire vegetable in your meal means less waste as well!

Another group of plants we recommend is herbs and spices, if the climate allows. A simple herb garden can thrive in such a small space and provide tons of fresh, delicious flavor to your home. Chives are notoriously easy to grow, and they will resprout each season with almost no work. Basil, cilantro, mint, and rosemary are also great candidates for your herb garden. Keep these in a small space with lots of sunlight and give them lots of water, but be careful not to overwater them. Parsley and dill also grow fast and fruitful and are great for adding to marinades and brines.

Growing certain types of flowers on your homestead can also be quite beneficial. Though they may not be edible, planting flowers with pollen that attracts honey bees is a great way to help grow your plants stronger through the natural process of cross-pollination from the bees. Attracting bees to your homestead will allow them to thrive in their bee community, and the pollen they drop as they fly through can strengthen the growth of certain other plants on your homestead. Also, growing sunflowers is especially good for homestead-living, as they not only attract bees but also provide you with sun flower seeds. These seeds, along with grains from your corn and other crops, can be used as bird feed if you are raising chickens and are also good for other plant-eating animals that may be on your homestead.

EASIEST CROPS FOR YOUR HOMESTEAD

Most of the crops we have already mentioned are pretty easy to grow. Potatoes and other root vegetables like winter squash; really all the essentials are not going to be too tough. We know that you are just starting off your homestead, however, and you may be looking for some other easy crop options that will grow well and don't require too much work while you get settled and figure out homestead life. Not to worry; there are so many options available and so many hearty crops that grow in any conditions. You will be moving on to fancy, complicated farming techniques in no time. Meanwhile, here are some of the easier crops to grow on your homestead that we recommend.

One great opportunity is peanuts. These legumes are relatively easy to grow and thrive in warmer climates, but can survive in the cold as well. They are also home to nitrogen-fixing bacteria that can keep up the fertility in your garden. Peanuts are full of protein and easy to store, plus they are a delicious snack—great for any occasion!

Another crop you may want to check out is quinoa or amaranth. Closely related to rice, these grains are protein-dense and basically grow like weeds. Once you plant them, they will sprout up everywhere. Quinoa is better for colder climates while amaranth thrives in warmer areas, so you can try your hand at either depending on where your homestead is situated.

Red raspberries are a delicious summer treat that can serve so many purposes: eaten fresh, preserved in jam, or baked into pastries. You can even add the leaves to your salads or brew them into a delicious tea that can relieve some muscle pain and cramps. They grow wild with little care in the summer and warmer season, and they sprout up little shoots that can be dug up and transplanted easily. Thus, you can save your crop for the next season and even replenish or increase your yield with minimal effort.

Another delicious berry you can try your hand at is straw berries. Similar to raspberries, these little guys grow wild and have so many benefits. Strawberry plants are usually the first to sprout in the springtime, providing you with much needed vitamin C. Strawberry plants even have some medicinal properties and can be brewed into tea that can relieve digestive issues such as diarrhea. They are perennial, and each year, they send out runners so that the patch can easily be replenished every season.

On the topic of medicinal plants, Aloe Vera is another great one to grow. Being a common houseplant, it can survive in many conditions as long as it is properly looked after and thrives in warmer climates. Aloe Vera also has many healing properties, specifically for skin as the inside contains a gel-like substance that is great for cooling and pain-relief on rashes and burns. Aloe plants are constantly shooting up clones to repopulate that you can transplant, and it requires little watering or fertilization.

OPTIMIZING YOUR CROP GROWTH

Regardless of what crops you are growing, optimizing your system is so important for a successful homestead. You want to be able to use your space and resources wisely and with as little waste as possible. Being a sustainable homestead means making use of all your resources and leaving little leftover that goes unused.

There are a lot of different ways to optimize your homestead, especially when it comes to crop growth. One key example is crop placement. There are many plants that you will be growing on your homestead that can do better or worse depending on what is around them. Whichever plants you choose to grow, do some research into which other plants are compatible. It is possible that planting two crops next to each other can form a symbiotic relationship in which both are mutually benefiting from each other's close presence.

It is also important to understand hydroponics and aquaponics so that you have a successful irrigation system in place. Your plants need to be well-watered, without going overboard. You don't want to overwater as it can ruin your crops, and it is a waste of a natural resource. You also don't want to be under watering and let your crops dry out and die, however, so it is important to know exactly how much water to be giving each of your plants and how often, as well as what system works best for your homestead.

HYDROPONICS

Hydroponics is a way of growing your crops without soil and instead using a liquid solvent. There can be many benefits to hydroponics, and you may want to consider using this technique on your homestead. At home, hydroponics is not as complicated as it sounds, and depending on how much space you have for your homestead, it may be the right method for you.

Hydroponics uses a mineral, nutrient-dense solution that can come from many different sources to grow crops completely without soil. Many plants such as tomatoes, peppers, cucumbers, and lettuces can be easily-grown hydroponically, clearing up space outside for other crops you may be growing. There are many advantages to hydroponic farming, including the notable decrease in the amount of water necessary. This makes it possible to grow crops in harsh conditions where you may not have access to as much water.

To create a hydroponic system, we recommend you first set up a greenhouse, although it is not necessary. There are a few different ways to set up a hydroponics system at home, and you may need to adjust some of these parts to suit your homestead. For the most part, all you need to create your own at-home hydroponics system is a table or wooden stand on which you will grow your crops, waste pipes to house the water, PVC pipes to connect them together, and a hose with a pump to keep the running water flowing through the pipes. You will also want a large container for the storage of output water. The only other elements you will need are fresh water, oxygen, root support, nutrients, and lots of light.

First, set up the space where you are going to grow your crops. Then, fill a large storage bin with water and mineral nutrient solution. This is what your plants will use to grow strong. Next, using a drill with a rotary circle cutter or hole saw drill bit, cut three inch holes through your waste pipe at approximately seven inches apart. Make sure that the holes you cut are all straight and even on the pipe, as this is where your plants will grow up once the system is in place. Set up your waste pipes on a flat surface in rows. How many rows and how long they are is up to you and will depend on the space you have on your homestead. Once they are laid out, you can use PVC pipe to connect the waste pipes on the end. Make sure all of them are connected in a way that will create one long tube essentially which the water can flow through. At one end, you will insert your hose where the fresh, nutrient-rich water will flow through the entire system. At the other end, you have a tube that drains the water back into the storage bin to be reused.

For a hydroponics system such as this one we recommend, you get a fountain pump that can run continuously without needing to be turned on or off. Connect it to the hose to push the water through your pipes and make sure that your output hose is secure to the water reservoir. You don't want to go out to check on your crops and see that they've all dried up because of a misplaced hose.

AQUAPONICS

Aquaponics is a step past hydroponics, which combines your water-based, soilless crops with aquaculture; or the raising of fish and other marine life. Aquaponics works to use both fields in a symbiotic relationship to enhance your crops' growth and improve the conditions of the fish. If you are thinking of rearing fish on your homestead, I highly recommend using aquaponics to not only improve the system, but also to save space and optimize the growth of your crops and animals on your homestead. Growing fish and vegetables together is more complicated, as it does involve more moving parts and living creatures to care for, but if you have the time and space, it is worth it.

Luckily, if you understand hydroponics, you are pretty much halfway to aquaponics already. The only difference on the vegetable side of things is that instead of a small storage bin water reservoir, you are going to need a big space where you store your water as that is where your fish will live. As you take care of your fish, they will supply the water with important nutrients that are great for vegetation growth, just like in nature. Aquaponics also relies on a closed system of water, so there is no runoff or waste of any kind.

There are so many benefits to aquaponics for both you and your homestead and its reduced environmental impact. An aquaponics system can cut down so many garden chores, as it eliminates watering and weeding completely. It also saves space in the long run as a small aquaponics system can replace a large plot of land that would be needed to grow your crops. It is a completely natural ecosystem with no added chemicals or pesticides and can be set up almost anywhere. An aquaponics system is also scalable, and you can have a smaller or larger setup depending on how much space you have on your homestead.

The only part of aquaponics we haven't been over is caring for your fish. Just like any plant or other animal, you will have to take care of your fish and tend to them daily to make sure they are growing strong and healthy. Whether you just keep them as pets or plan on using the fish for food, make sure you feed them appropriately and keep their tank or basin clean of any mold or algae that may start to crop up. The fish are going to be feeding your plants, so regardless of if you plan on using them for food or not, make sure they are healthy and have good living conditions. We suggest using freshwater fish such as tilapia or barramundi in your aquaponics system, as they grow fast and can tolerate diverse conditions. Other good options include trout in lower water temperatures, and you can even add other aquatic life such as snails and shrimp to your system.

Aquaponics may be a little more complicated, but once the setup is complete, most of the hard work is as well. Taking care of your vegetables will require the same efforts as any other hydroponics system and even less than a regular gardening method. Taking care of the marine life generally just means paying extra attention and spending extra time to make sure their water is clean and fresh, and that they are well-fed, healthy, and not over or under populating the tank. With the huge variety of benefits, there is no reason not to try your hand at this great method to improve your homestead!

CHAPTER 4
PRESERVING EVERYTHING

Now that you know the basics of growing your own crops, it's time to learn about preserving and storing them. It's one thing to have all this homegrown food, but if you don't know proper preservation techniques, it can go bad quickly and all your hard work will be for naught. Homesteading encompasses more than just growing your own food; it is a lifestyle. Homesteading means tending to the land, taking care of it, and preserving what you take from it and giving back in order to live in harmony with the earth. Once you understand the art of growing, preserving, storing, and eventually, eating, you can extrapolate these ideals to the rest of your life, and that is when you will truly be a homesteader.

There are many ways in which you can preserve both the crops you grow and the meat from animals you raise, as well as ways to use every part of the plant or animal, to ensure almost nothing goes to waste. Done properly, homesteading can have little to no negative environmental impact, and you can save and store your homegrown goods to last you as long as you need. Preserving your food is especially important for the wintertime when you may be unable to grow crops, meaning you'll need to store up as much as you can during the summer if you want to survive out on your own.

CANNING FOOD

If done properly, canning food is a safe and effective method at storing your goods and keeping them fresh for longer. The process involves placing food in jars and sealing them so that no microorganisms or bacteria can get in and cause the food to spoil. Canning can also deactivate enzymes in the food that cause it to spoil when left out in the open for long periods of time. This allows you to keep food fresh for as long as you may need, and when it comes time to use, you can simply open a jar.

If your canning process is not done properly, it can cause the food to rot, or worse, have dangerous health effects. Microorganisms that you are unable to see can grow inside your canned food without your knowledge, and some of them are harmful to humans when consumed. One example is the Clostridium botulinum bacteria, which can grow and release spores in your food. This bacteria is the cause of botulism, and if the spores are left to grow, then they can produce a deadly botulinum toxin. It is very important when canning your food to ensure that you have thoroughly researched the best method to can that specific item.

So, what are some canning methods? Let's go over a few. In general, there are three main ways to safely can your goods: a boiling water bath method, an atmospheric steam canning method, and the pressure canning method. Which method you use will vary depending on what you are trying to preserve, but you should always be following one of these methods.

BOILING WATER BATH METHOD

This method of canning is best for fruits, jams, and jellies, as well as tomatoes and pickles. The process involves jarring and sealing your foods, then dipping the jars into a pot of water and bringing it to a boil. You want to be sure that the jar is completely submerged during this process, so that every inch is heated correctly. By bringing the water to a boil, you will kill any bacteria or spores that may have been growing on your food, as they cannot survive at high temperatures.

For this method to work correctly, you must be sure that the water level is at approximately one inch above the lid of the jar. Once the water comes to a boil, keep it heated for at least 10 minutes or whatever the recommended processing time is for the food you are preserving. Once the processing time has passed, turn off the heat and let the jars sit in the water for five minutes or longer before you go to remove them. Carefully place the jars on a cooling rack and leave them there for 12-24 hours. Don't touch or try to adjust the lid or any part of the jar until they have completely cooled. Once the jars have cooled, you can check that they are properly sealed. If they are, then you can proceed to storing them. If you find that the jar is not sealed properly, do not try to adjust the lid, as breaking the seal cannot be undone. Instead, take the jar, and place it in the fridge to consume within a few days.

This method works great for high-acid foods with a pH balance below 4.6 with no extra work needed. Foods such as fruits and properly pickled vegetables fall into this category. For low-acid foods such as tomatoes and figs which have a pH value closer to 4.6, an acidic solution must be added to ensure that the bacteria will be completely killed off. Add a few spoons of lemon juice or citric acid to your jar to ensure that all the spores are killed, and your food is safely preserved.

ATMOSPHERIC STEAM CANNING METHOD

The second method of canning is good for naturally acidic or properly acidified foods such as fruits, preservatives, and pickled vegetables. This method should not be used for low acid foods such as vegetables or meat. The reason being similar to that of the previous method: you want to ensure that any bacteria or spores that may be within the jar are properly neutralized and killed. With a steam canner, you cannot add acidic liquid to the steam, so only use this method for foods that are high-acid.

The steam canner works similarly to the boiling bath method. The jars are placed on a rack above a reservoir of water, and the steam created from the boiling water provides a thermal treatment for the jars. This method uses less water and can be a lot faster than the boiling bath method. The steam canner also requires less energy and time to reach its peak point, at which the jars are safely preserved.

For this method to work best, preheat the jars before you put them into the steam canner, and try to minimize cooling before the process can occur. Once the jars are in the steam canner properly, allow the full processing time to pass. Once they have been properly processed, turn off the heat and carefully remove the lid of the steam canner. Do not touch the jars for at least five minutes while they cool off a bit. Afterwards, move the jars to a cooling rack, just as in the previous method, and allow them to sit for 12-24 hours before checking that they've been properly sealed.

PRESSURE CANNING METHOD

The third and final canning method is pressure canning. This is the only method that is safe and functional for low-acid foods such as vegetables, meat, poultry, and seafood. Due to the dangers of botulism and these bacteria, these foods must be canned using a pressure canner. The jars of food you want to preserve must be placed in a couple inches of water and boiled to at least 240°F. This level of heat can only be reached by a pressure canner.

To use the pressure canner, prep your jars and place them into the canner with two to three inches of water surrounding the bottom. The water should be hot but not yet boiling. Once the jars are all properly placed, shut the lid to the canner and make sure the steam cannot escape except through the vent. Turn heat on high, and once the steam begins to escape through the vent of the pressure canner, let it escape steadily for 10 or so minutes. After that, close the vent to create the pressure within the canner. Some pressure canners will allow you to control the amount of pressure placed and some you will have to monitor yourself. Allow the pressure to rise to the correct amount as recommended, and then turn the heat down slightly to maintain that level. Once the weight on the pressure canner begins to move slightly, begin counting the processing time. Once the processing time has elapsed, turn off the heat and remove the canner if you can. It will take about a half an hour for the pressure to return to zero, and once it has, you can remove the lid facing away from you so that the steam doesn't burn you when it escapes. Then, you can place your jars on a cooling rack and follow the same steps as with the other methods for storage.

PREPARING TO CAN

When you prepare to can your food, always gather your equipment first, get set up, and grab the food last. This ensures that the food is only sitting out for the shortest amount of time possible. Also, try to follow these preservation methods only on foods that are properly ripened and not overly ripe. You also don't want to overdo it. Only gather as much as you will be able to handle in two or three hours. If you gather too much food and have it sitting out for too long while you are working, some of it will slowly start to go bad before you can even get it in the containers.

When you gather your jars and lids, inspect them individually to ensure that there are no cracks or breaks and that all of them seal properly. Wash them thoroughly, and try to keep them warm. Keeping the jars warm when you add the food will prevent any breaks during the canning process. You should also be sure to use two-piece lids as they are safest and work best.

There are a couple different ways to pack your jars. First is raw packing. This is where you put the food directly into the jar without any other prep. For this method, be sure to pack foods into the jar as tightly as you can, as most foods will shrink during the process. The exception is for corn, beans, potatoes, and peas, as they actually expand during canning. After you've packed the food into the jar, add boiling water, juice, or warmed syrup over the food until it is all completely covered. Anywhere between a half a cup to 1½ cups of water should be good for a quart jar.

The second method is to hot-pack your jars. This simply means that you heat your food first by either boiling it or cooking it before adding it to the jars with the boiling liquid. In this process, the food will have already undergone the shrinkage from the heat, so you can pack the jars just loosely enough to allow the liquid to fully submerge the food inside. Then, same as before, seal your jar with the lid and make sure it is nice and tight.

When adding your food to the jars, keep the area and jars as clean as possible. Then, you can add your jars to the water or steam canner and begin boiling. Make sure to leave the jars in the boiling water or steam canner for at least 10 minutes. This is to ensure that they are properly sterilized during the process. Then, remove the jars carefully and try not to burn yourself, and it's on to storage.

Most two-piece jars will make a 'pop' noise when you tap on the lid if they are sealed properly. While the jars are cooling, this is your indicator on whether or not they have been properly sealed. If you don't hear the noise, refrigerate the jar and use the food within two to three days. Jars that are properly sealed can be stored for extended periods of time. When you put your jars in storage, try to organize them with the ones containing the least liquid at the front. These will be the ones you want to make a note to use first.

It is best to store your canned food in a clean, cool, dry, and dark place, such as a basement or cellar. Ideal temperature is between 50 and 70°F. Canned food left in the sun or in hot conditions will spoil faster; same with damp conditions where water may corrode the lids and cause rust. Once you have your jars in a dry, cool place, you can keep them stored for around a year. Depending on what you are storing, they may last longer or shorter, but generally, the rule of thumb is to use your stores by the one-year mark.

DRYING FOOD

Another option for preserving your food is dehydration or drying it out. This simple method ensures that your food stays good for longer and can be extremely beneficial for life on the homestead. By dehydrating your food, you effectively remove any water from it and can prevent it from spoiling for pretty much forever. Drying food for preservation has actually been used by humans for thousands and thousands of years!

There are many advantages to preserving food through dehydration. Just like with canning, dried foods can be stored in a dark, cool place without any electricity or power necessary. Since they no longer have any water, most bacteria will die off immediately as they cannot generally survive without water. Drying foods also brings out new flavors that you may have never tried before. If you have ever eaten raisins, you know that they taste nothing like the grapes they once were.

There are a variety of different ways to dry food, and the method you choose will depend on what kind of food you are drying. One popular way is to use a smoker for meats and fish. If you have an oven that goes to a low enough temperature, you can even dry out your goods right on the top rack. The trick to drying out food, especially meats and fish, is that the temperature must be hot enough for the water to evaporate from the food, but not so much as to 'cook' the food. Cooking involves heating food to a degree in which the chemical com position of the food is changed in the process. This is what you DON'T want to happen in the dehydration practice!

Smoking meat can refer to two different things: preserving it or barbequing it. We will obviously be focusing on the preservation aspect of a smoker. Smoking meat is effectively cooking it at very low temperatures for an extended period of time in order to slowly dehydrate it without losing any of the delicious flavor and important nutrients. This method of food preservation has been used by humans for ages.

For most fruits and vegetables, you can just lay them out in the sun on a flat, dry surface to dry them out. Many herbs and some kinds of vegetables can simply be hung to dry. On hot sunny days, you can easily lay out a blanket or mat and dry out your fruits and veggies. You can also buy a special mat that enhances the process or make your own using aluminum foil. The foil catches the sunlight and reflects it, speeding up the drying process.

If you live in an area where hot, sunny days are not as reliable, you may want to invest in an electric dehydration machine or something similar. Excess humidity can also cause foods to mold quickly, so using an electric dehydrator is great for cloudy or rainy days. Regardless of how you dry your food, make sure you wash it thoroughly first so that it is nice and clean. You also may have to blanch your fruits and vegetables by dipping them in lemon juice or citric acid before dehydrating them in order to preserve their color and flavor. For most foods, you will need to cut everything into small, uniform pieces before using a dehydration machine. This goes for fruits, vegetables, and meats as well, and be sure to remove any fatty sections of the meat before drying it. Cutting your fruits and veggies into small pieces can also be useful for letting them dry in the sunlight, as the increased surface area can slightly speed up the process.

To store your dehydrated foods, first allow them to cool before packing them in airtight containers or plastic bags. Dried foods should always be stored in a cool, dry, dark place, just like canned foods. This is to optimize the preservation and avoid having the food spoil due to heat or water damage. Dehydrated food can generally last between six months to a year in storage.

THE ART OF HOMESTEADING

Preserving is not just about food. To truly live a homestead lifestyle, the values of preservation and recycling must be transferred from simple food storage methods to an entire mindset and way of living. Once you start your homestead, you will begin to look at everything you own and wonder how it can be reused and upcycled. Our goal with teaching you to homestead is to change your way of thinking, so that you can see how to be more sustainable in every aspect of your life!

By the time you start working on your homestead, you should be looking to shift your mindset from the capitalist society to which you may be accustomed, to a sustainable, agrarian perspective on life. Think about what you need, not what you want. Consider the land your partner, not your property, and your homestead is not just a way to make food yourself, but a way to sustain you, your family, and even your community through sustainable practices. On the homestead, hard work, focus, and skill is what's going to keep you going, not money and materials. We want you to be able to shift your mindset more towards "make do or do without" and away from unsustainable, consumerist ideals that harm our planet.

Historically, homesteading was a way of living; and not just any way of living, but it was the only way. Now, over time and progress, we have all the resources we need available at our fingertips, and it has made us lazy and naive as a society. Homesteading connected us to the earth, to our food, and to our families and communities. The way we live now, in a society run by capitalism and consumerism, we are losing those connections, and what's worse, we are destroying the earth. We can still get back to the good life, though, through hard work, commitment, and determination.

Homesteading can bring us back to what's important, and that in itself is art.

Building up your homestead can show others that this way of living is not only feasible, but highly successful and fulfilling. It may require more direct work to satisfy your needs, but it is so much more rewarding than anything else I have ever done. Through your homestead, you can create a community. Find others who have similar values to you, teach those around you about the joys of this life, and raise your locality up to the standards of preservation and sustainability we are trying to achieve.

When we talk about preservation, we don't just mean preserving food so that you have some saved for later. We are talking about the preservation and reuse of everything you have. Old tools can be taken apart and used to build something new, scraps and leftovers can be composted or fed to animals, and excess materials can be used for new projects or given to those in need. To truly be living the homestead lifestyle is to be 100 percent sustainable in your life so that you leave no garbage behind. It seems like a hard task at first, but once you start thinking of homesteading as a way of living, you will be able to accept that you can do anything.

Learn to apply these preservation skills and values to all aspects of your life. For example, preserve cheese by creating a wax seal around it, similar to canning your food. Try your hand at salt curing meats to help them last longer without using electricity or power. You can make homemade cheese in a DIY cheese press, homemade oils, vinegars, and more, and you can even learn to build an outdoor oven using stones and bricks or learn how to bake food without an oven at all. There are so many ways to constantly be improving, upgrading, and outdoing yourself and your homestead, and that's the beauty of it. You will never reach the perfect level or have the perfect homestead because there are always ways to do better!

CHAPTER 5
CREATING A TRULY
OPTIMIZED SYSTEM

Now that your homestead is set up, and you've started growing and preserving, the next step is to optimize your homestead. Optimizing the processes on your homestead can take you to the next level, from growing your own food to becoming a truly sustainable homestead. You have only just started your journey to sustainable living, and in this next chapter, we are going to discuss all the ways you can integrate this new mindset into all aspects of your life.

COMPOSTING

We've discussed composting a few times already. However, it's time to go into some important details. Why should you compost? Well first of all, composting is just a way of recycling organic materials. Instead of putting scraps in the garbage and having them get sent off to a dump or landfill that will promote pollution, composting organic leftovers gives it new life. Organic materials such as food and yard waste can contribute to up to 50 percent of the average household trash. Reducing your waste by up to 50 percent is huge! Remember, homesteading is all about reusing materials and wasting as little as possible, and composting organic scraps is part of that outlook.

Composting can reduce your carbon footprint, and it can also benefit your homestead directly. When organic material breaks down, it becomes a great natural fertilizer for your garden. Adding compost to the soil where your crops grow promotes strong and healthy plant growth through a multitude of different functions.

Composting is a great way to take your homestead to the next level, and on top of that, it helps to reduce greenhouse gases on a larger scale as well. It can be hard to take a look at the bigger picture sometimes and step outside our small view of the world, but if we want to live sustainably and treat the earth right, we *must*. When you put out your trash bin at the corner on garbage day, you may not think about where that garbage goes: off to some dump somewhere. Not only do these huge dumps and landfills contribute to pollution, but the trucks that carry all the trash are also emitting carbon dioxide and other gases into the air, polluting our environment even further.

First of all, compost can increase the organic materials in your soil. This will make the soil more nutrient-dense and can help the plants better absorb these nutrients. Adding compost to your soil can also strengthen plant growth by keeping the soil pH levels balanced. Not only that, but adding compost to soil can also make clay-like soils more airy and easier to work with, while making sandier soils better equipped to retain water. Compost can even help regulate soil temperatures by insulating the soil around the plants. Using your compost as a natural fertilizer for your crops is especially good, because unlike store-bought fertilizers, compost will naturally regulate and release nutrients into the soil slowly and at a steady pace. It also won't harm any of your plants like some chemical fertilizers can.

One way to upgrade your compost game is to add worms into the mix. 'Vermicompost', as it's called when worms are introduced into the compost system, is especially good for homestead life, as it provides many more benefits. On top of all the already mentioned benefits of composting, vermicomposting speeds up the process by which the organic materials are broken down and turned to fertilizer. Not only that, but the compost which the worms create can be used in a concentrated form as a natural weed killer, keeping your homestead clear of any invasive plants that could threaten to overrun your crops.

MAKING THE PERFECT COMPOST

Creating a great, natural compost right in your backyard is super simple. The only materials you will need beforehand are a large bin with a lid and some organic matter to get it started. A good compost is layered with a mix of brown and green organic materials and sits out on a flat surface that faces the sun. Heat from the sun can help your scraps decompose faster, so you won't have to wait as long before using it as fertilizer.

Once you've found a spot for your compost bin, start with a first layer of coarse, brown materials. Things like twigs and sticks; paper egg cartons if you have them. This bottom layer will help with water drainage and keep the bottom of your bin from getting moldy. The next layer should be dry and flat. We recommend you cover the surface of the coarse layer with dried leaves and newspaper. After that, alternate between brown layers, which are going to be carbon-based materials, and green layers of nitrogen-based materials. Some great brown compost materials include pine needles, dried leaves and sticks, dried grass clippings and yard waste, paper towels and napkins, bits of cardboard, shredded, brown paper bags, and more. For green compost materials, try using green leaves and garden waste, egg shells, scraps of fruits and vegetables, tea bags and coffee grounds, and even flowers.

Once you've set up the first few layers of your compost, you can leave it be. As you collect waste from your kitchen and yard, add it to your compost bin, making sure to add layers of brown as well. One great trick to remembering to toss your scraps in the compost is by keeping a smaller compost bin in your kitchen under the sink or in another place where the smell won't bother you or attract bugs. You can dump all your leftovers and scraps into the small bin or container, and once it fills up, transfer it to your compost bin. Keep adding to your compost bin until it is full.

As the compost decomposes, the materials in the bin will shrink. Make sure that when you are adding materials to the bin, you mix them in properly with the layers near the bottom so that it decomposes all evenly. Your compost should maintain a balanced level of moisture, meaning you may need to add some water if it is too dry or wring out materials that are waterlogged before mixing them into the heap. Be sure to mix or flip your compost every week or so to keep it even, help the process of breaking down the materials, and eliminate any odor.

You will know the compost is complete when it is dark and has a crumbly, earthy texture. It should look and smell similar to soil. Finished compost will usually have risen to the top of the bin, so you can easily remove it. Remove the finished compost, taking care to leave anything that has not finished in the bin to continue decomposing. Then, you can use the finished compost as fertilizer.

There are a few things you should be wary NOT to compost, as they could prevent the process or even harm your garden. Avoid adding any meats, oils, or grease to your compost bin, as they will not decompose along with the rest of the materials.

Any weeds that you pull from your yard should also stay separated from your compost, as they generally reproduce by dropping seeds everywhere, and could start growing right in your compost bin. Obviously, any plant materials that are diseased or moldy should not be added to the compost, either, at the risk of ruining the entire bin, and any wood chips or sawdust from pressure-treated wood should be avoided as well. Dairy products are also a huge no-go for your compost, as they decompose differently from the rest of these materials, and they don't smell so great either.

COMPANION PLANTING

Companion planting is a great way to optimize your homestead and highly effective at promoting healthy crop growth. Companion planting is essentially just growing two or more species of crops next to or near each other in order for the plants to form a symbiotic relationship and benefit from each other's close presence. It may seem silly to say that plants can have best friends that make them better, but really, companion planting is just a gardening strategy that promotes growth by putting mutually beneficial plants near each other.

How does companion planting work, you wonder? Well, there are a variety of reasons two plants may benefit from being near each other. Growing a nitrogen-fixing plant next to a nonnitrogen-fixing plant can help balance soil fertility and promote growth for both plants. Large plants can often be used as natural trellises for smaller plants that require one. A tall plant can easily provide scaffolding for a smaller, climbing plant to grow upon. Large plants can also be used to regulate sunlight and heat for smaller plants that may thrive better in the shadow of their larger partner. A companion plant may even be able to keep away pests by masking their partner or confusing the pests that may be nearby. There are so many benefits to companion planting, and when done correctly, it can take your homestead to the next level.

The most well-known example of companion planting is the "Three Sister" trio of corn or maize, climbing beans, and winter squash. This trio was often grown together by Native American communities due to their complementary nature, and the practice has since been passed on to homesteaders and gardeners far and wide. The tall corn can support the climbing beans, and the winter squash protects the soil around the plants from too much moisture or heat. The big, prickly leaves of the squash also prevent pests from making their home in your plants and discourage weed growth as well. Climbing beans are also a nitrogen-fixing plant and pretty fast-growing, so they provide nitrogen for the corn and squash as all three grow together.

Obviously, corn and beans are a great pair as already mentioned, but there are so many other pairings and companion plants of which you can make use. Tomatoes and carrots, for example; the tomatoes provide shade and pest control while the carrots grow underground and aerate the soil. Planting chives near your lettuce and spinach can repel pests that are naturally attracted to leafy greens. Herbs are especially useful as companion plants, as many of them have properties that deter pests and discourage weed growth. Basil, parsley, and borage all pair well with tomatoes, as they repel or distract many pests from going near the tomatoes and attract bees to improve pollination. Another great companion plant for beans and cucumbers is sunflowers, as they grow tall and strong and can provide shade as they always face the sun.

Companion planting can be tricky at first, but once you get the hang of it, the benefits are innumerable. Once you find yourself getting into the rhythm of your homesteading life, try some of these combinations we mentioned and watch how your plants flourish. After a while, companion planting will become second nature to you, and you'll even be able to come up with your own combinations that you discover work well together.

BEEHIVES

Beehives are another amazing way to increase productivity on your homestead and promote sustainability in congruity with Mother Nature. Bees are incredible animals that can improve your homestead exponentially. It takes just as much work to care for a beehive as it does to care for your veggies, possibly even less, and the bees will help your crops thrive. Plus, you can harvest honey from the bees regularly that you can then store or sell for some extra profit.

Before getting started with your bee colony, take into account a few different factors. First, research the laws and regulations surrounding beekeeping in your area. Certain regions have limits on how many colonies you can keep in a certain amount of space. Plus, if you are working with limited space, be sure to consult your family, neighbors, and anyone else who may be affected by your bees. You are going to need a place to keep them. Beyond just outside in your yard or garden, your bee colony should be kept off the ground so as to dissuade any wild animals from going near it. Keeping the boxes up above ground on a bench or a stand made of cement blocks works, although you may want something more permanent depending on the scope of your homestead.

To care for a bee colony on your homestead, there are a few things you will need. First, a bee box. You can purchase one from specialized garden centers and stores or online, or you can always make one yourself. If you are going to build your own bee box, make sure to do your research beforehand, as you want to build a space where the colony can survive and thrive. Bee boxes are relatively simple to build yourself, and the only materials you will need are some plywood, a few boards, some trim-head screws, and a sheet of aluminum flashing. You'll also need some sheets of beeswax to help get the colony started. Making your own beehive box is not a difficult project, but there are quite a few intricate steps that need to be followed, so make sure you are prepared for the commitment.

If you aren't looking to raise your own colony just yet, but still want to attract bees to your homestead for their pollinator powers, try building a DIY beehouse. A beehouse is a little different from a beehive or box in that it isn't made to house an entire colony, but rather individual bees as they come through. Your native species of cavity-resting bees will be encouraged to come to your homestead and pollinate, mate, and even reproduce if you have a beehouse on your property. A beehouse with a variety of little tunnels, chambers, nooks, and crannies is the perfect spot for bees to rest between pollination and even find a mate with which to reproduce.

Though bumblebees form colonies with a queen, many species of bees are actually solitary and live their life without a queen or colony. They nest in small cavities and do not produce honey, but still greatly contribute to the pollination of our gardens and farms. These bees include digger bees, miner bees, sweat bees, squash bees, and blueberry bees, which are all ground-nesters. There are also mason bees and leaf-cutter bees that nest in hollow tunnels in trees or dead wood. These bees will build nests, lay their eggs, and seal it off once they mate. If you can provide a spot for these bees to mate and lay their eggs with a beehouse, the baby bees will all grow up on your homestead, attracting more bees with which to mate and providing free pollination for your crops.

To make a beehouse, all you need is a large frame and material that will provide a variety of different sizes and depths of tunnels or compartments for the bees. For your frame, you can build one out of spare planks of wood or reuse an old crate. Pieces of tree bark and hollowed branches, wooden blocks that you've hollowed out with a drill, and even old paper towel rolls or toilet paper rolls can be used to create the tunnels where the bees will rest and nest. When you put your beehouse together, make sure that the tunnels and compartments vary in size, length, and width so that the bees can have their pick. You can use twigs and branches, dried leaves, pine cones, and string or twine to tie it all together and keep the structure sturdy.

Beehouse maintenance is very simple. First of all, you don't want to use any pressure-treated wood in the house, as it may not be good for the bees. Try not to introduce any chemicals that may be harmful. To keep the beehouse clean, make sure to replace the wooden tunnels or paper tubes every year or so.

The best way to attract native pollinators is to grow native species of plants. Do some research on your local area, and find out which flowers or other plants are bee-attractors. Many native bees are specialists and only go after specific plants, so research is key here. Another tip is to add a sandbox to your garden near the beehouse. This will give ground-nesting bees a place to store their food and other resources. You should also add a source of water for your bees. A small tray or even pet bowl will work; just add some rocks and pebbles for the bees to sit on while they hydrate. Most importantly, avoid the use of pesticides on your homestead at all costs. Find other ways to keep pests from rooting around your vegetables, as pesticides can be harmful to the good bugs as well.

FARM ANIMALS

Keeping animals on your homestead can be a lot of hard work, but it is also a great way to keep up your sustainability goals and keep your homestead active. Many animals also naturally produce food sources, such as chickens with their eggs, and the meat from these farm animals can keep you going through the wintertime. Keeping animals on your homestead is a great way to increase productivity, improve your self-reliance, and earn some extra profit.

CHICKENS

Chickens are probably the easiest animals to keep on your homestead. They take up relatively little space, are cheap to feed (especially if you grow corn or plants with a lot of excess seeds), and they produce eggs! They are outdoor birds that historically lived in forests, jungles, and fields and can survive well in almost any weather. Most of the work it takes to raise chickens is really just common sense. You need to feed them, keep their coop clean, and make sure they have enough space to go about their business.

There are really just three essential steps for caring for chickens: housing and shelter, food and water, and space. General convention says that a chicken house needs about one square foot of floor area per chicken. We recommend you go a little bigger if you have the space, especially if you plan on raising more than four or five chickens. The more you have, the messier that house is going to get. Building your own chicken house and coop is relatively simple, as they don't need many complex structures; just a shelter with nesting boxes and enough space for the chickens to rest comfortably.

Chickens live healthier and longer when they have a clean, secure shelter. They also naturally seek out shelter and protection when the sun sets, so having a house for your chickens to nest in is a necessity. While there are other options, such as pet cages and even free-range living, having a chicken house with a run is generally the best option for homestead living. This will keep your chickens safe from predators, provide them with a shelter that you can easily access and clean, and give them enough space to roam around without losing track of them. Fencing off an area for your chicken coop is easy enough, and building a chicken house yourself is a cheaper alternative to buying; that is not as complex as many other homestead projects.

To build your chicken house, you're going to need to keep a couple of things in mind. First, as already mentioned, make sure you build big enough to comfortably house all your chickens. For beginners, keeping track of more than four or five chickens can quickly become a lot to handle, so a small house with just a few residents is probably your best bet. Most chicken houses are also raised above ground, either on stilts or on a deck. This keeps the house clean from the dirt and moisture of the ground that could get in and not only dirty the chicken house, but also compromise the structure if it becomes moldy. You also want to avoid any cold or damp conditions within the chicken house as the chickens won't like it and could even become sick.

Aside from building a simple shed-like structure to house your chickens, you will also need nest boxes within the house. This is where your chickens rest and lay their eggs. To build a nest box is quite simple, as they are essentially just small compartments where your hens will go when they lay their eggs. Take or build a small wooden box of about two square inches, with a seven or eight inch perch on which the hens can sit. Make sure your nesting boxes are easy to handle, as you will need to remove and replace them into the chicken house often. All you need to do is fill the boxes with a layer of hay or straw for cushioning, and you're done! The perches should be a little higher than the nest boxes to prevent the birds from sleeping in them. Keep the nest boxes in a darker corner of the chicken house for privacy, so the hens will not be disturbed while laying their eggs.

To feed your chickens, keep a feeder full and accessible at all times, as well as a bowl or feeder of clean, fresh water. The feeder and water don't have to be placed within the chicken house, as the bird will likely knock them over often or contaminate the food and water, which will require cleaning. One hen will eat approximately 150g to 180g of feed pellets a day, so use that as the basis to add the right amount of feed for the number of chickens you are raising. Only provide them with enough food for two or three days at a time so as not to overfeed them, and the pellets will get stale and moldy after a few days. You can give your chickens corn, seeds, and even some green vegetables such as cabbage or cauliflower leaves as a treat in the afternoons, but don't feed them too much of this option, as they are not healthy for the chickens in excess.

GOATS

Goats are a great homestead animal as they are easier to care for than many others, can provide both dairy and meat, and take up less space, food, and water than a cow would. Raising homestead goats is a perfect way to become more connected with your food sources and with the earth. Goats can provide milk for dairy products and meat, as well as benefit your homestead by helping with the workload. For example, they can carry a pack full of tools or equipment you may need, can clear away brush, and can even have endearing personalities that make them enjoyable companions.

The main thing to be concerned about with goats is space. Raising any animal will take up a sizable amount of acreage on your homestead, so it's important to do your research before making any decisions. Luckily, goats come in many different breeds, and there are larger ones that are good for hard work, and smaller ones such as the Nigerian Dwarf goat, which could be raised in your backyard. Regardless of what breed of goat you go with, they all require the same (and relatively simple) housing and food.

For shelter, goats don't require anything too elaborate. As long as they have a space that is dry, well-ventilated, draft-free, and protects them from the elements, they will be happy as can be. Whether it be a traditional barn or a simple three sided-shelter, that depends on you and your homestead. Whatever works best and is most suited to the space you have will be fine, as long as you keep this in consideration before acquiring the goat. You'll also need good fencing around the area you plan on keeping your goat(s), to keep them from running wild around your homestead and keep predators away.

For food and water, goats don't require much. A simple five gallon bucket of clean water will suffice for their drinking source, and you will only have to change it out or refill it every day or two depending on how big or how many goats you have. Goats love to eat from a variety of different plants, bushes, and shrubs, though most homesteads are not equipped to provide goats with the space they need for browsing. Feed them from a trough or bucket with good quality, dry grass or hay. If it is time to milk a doe, you may want to supplement their food with alfalfa leaves or other grains such as corn, oats, and barley, to provide them with some extra protein, vitamins, and minerals. Many minerals, especially salt, are very important for goat health, so you may want to consider giving your goat a salt lick stone. This is up to your discretion.

Aside from breeding goats for their milk and meat, there are so many other benefits to having goats on your homestead. They can improve your pasture as they eat just about any kind of plant if you let them. Goats actually love poison ivy, so if you ever find yourself with a poison ivy problem, this could be an easy solution. They will also eat weeds and other shrubbery you may want to clear away. Goat droppings can also be used directly in your garden as fertilizer and don't need to be composted first. Goats are a herd animal and live better, longer lives when kept together, so take that into consideration as well before you decide if you want them on your farm. It is likely you won't be able to keep just one, but will have at least two or three of these beauties running around.

PIGS

Raising pigs can be so rewarding, as it is often a challenge, but they are such loving creatures you won't even realize that you're doing hard work when you are around them. There are also many benefits to having pigs on your homestead, as they can eliminate waste and provide you with much-needed, protein-dense meat. Owning pigs isn't for everyone, but if you find yourself up to the challenge of taking on another animal in your homestead, this is the one we recommend.

The easiest part of raising pigs on your homestead is that they will eat just about anything. Make sure they have a clean supply of water in their pen and a trough to fill with food, and that's pretty much all there is to worry about. Pigs will eat any leftover scraps from your kitchen, and they can even eat dairy products, meaning milk and cheese won't go to waste. Feeding your pigs expired products is fine, too; as long as they aren't moldy or clearly diseased, it should be completely safe and healthy for them. If you plan on selling the meat from your pigs for profit, make sure you boil any leftover food you do give them for at least 30 minutes to be extra sure that any microorganisms or bacteria living in the food that could be harmful have been killed.

The only downside to pigs eating just about anything is that they have to poop A LOT. Now, pigs are actually a lot smarter than we believe and a lot cleaner than we give them credit for, believe it or not. They will generally designate a specific corner or section of the pen to do their business, while keeping the rest of their area exceptionally clean. That being said, the one corner that isn't clean will be very smelly and require daily cleaning by you. As I said, pigs are smart, which means that they may try to escape their pen every once and a while. Make sure that the fencing you use for the pigpen is sturdy and reliable and the gate has a complex lock that needs fine motor skills to open. Otherwise, you may wake up to see your whole field eaten up over night!

Having pigs on your homestead can also be beneficial to other animals. Pigs can actually keep your other animals healthy as parasites from other animals are unable to survive in pigs. This can be said about many animals, if you raise more than one species. Because pigs have a very different internal system than horses, cows, goats, and other farm animals, they are dead ends for any parasites. This can be done by letting the animals roam around in the same areas at different times. Letting the pigs graze after the goats are herded back into their pen will allow the pigs to eat up all the eggs or larvae from the goat parasites. The parasites will be unable to survive in the pigs' system and thus die off.

STAYING GROUNDED ON THE HOMESTEAD

Now that you've started optimizing your homestead and perfecting your life, what's next? Well, the truth is that it's the same as before. Continue to grow, to improve, to fail and succeed, and to try new things. Even if the farm is running smoothly, there are always ways to improve, and if you are focused solely on the physical aspects of your homestead and the outcomes of your work, then you aren't living a true homestead life. Without a calm and centered outlook, you won't be able to properly take care of your homestead, and without the mindset of sustainability and coexistence, you won't be able to live in harmony with your homestead.

The most important thing to remember when living on your homestead is to always remain grounded. Keeping your head clear and your mind focused is just as important to optimizing your homestead as adding compost or raising animals. Without the proper mindset, all you have is a bunch of tools and equipment and a big backyard. What does it mean to be 'grounded'? It means you are keeping yourself in the present, not worrying too much about the outcome, but focusing more on the process. Feel your purpose on the homestead, and trust yourself to stay on the right path.

Creating a space for mindfulness is so important when homesteading. You need to be able to adapt to changes around you and learn to take challenges as they come to you. Take breaks when you need to, and always take time to yourself and find pleasure in the simple things. Life can be hard sometimes, especially on a homestead when you feel like you are almost constantly working. Make sure you are taking time to practice mindfulness; remind yourself how lucky you are to be going through this experience, and be proud of yourself for every little victory.

Staying active is not difficult on the homestead, but make sure you are doing activities you enjoy for fun, not just working to tend to the homestead 24/7. Take breaks to read, write, sing, or do whatever it is you may find peaceful and relaxing. Remember that taking care of your mind is just as important as taking care of your body and your homestead. Always prioritize your mental and emotional well-being. If something seems too overwhelming, take a step back and reevaluate what it is you are doing and why. If you can't find a solution you like, it's okay to give up and try again another time. Your homestead can only thrive if you yourself are thriving as well.

CHAPTER 6
HOMESTEADING FOR
PROFIT

Now that you are living the homestead lifestyle, how can you continue to maintain the things you love in life, strive for abundance, and profit from all your hard work? There are countless ways to profit off of your homestead, and you shouldn't feel limited just because you've shifted your mindset to a more sustainable way of life. You can live sustainably and still have everything you've ever wanted; it just takes some hard work, some smart moves, and belief in your dreams. Don't feel cornered by the homesteading ideals of "simple living"; you can be a homesteader and a successful business person at the same time!

From selling food from your garden, to sewing your own clothes and making artisanal breads and jams, there are countless ways to profit from all the work you do on your homestead. All you need is a little push to kick-start your homestead business and take you from hobbyist to professional homesteader. First and foremost, you're already saving money if you're a homesteader, and you're doing it while saving the environment, too. You're already in control of your life, and you have all the tools necessary to start turning a profit.

SAVING MONEY

There are so many easy ways to save money on your homestead. Obviously, you are already growing your own crops, saving on food, and even raising animals to provide you with the essential protein your body needs. But how else can you save some cash while living your best homesteader life? Well, let's discuss some options! All you need to do is take that homesteading mindset you've been cultivating all this time and apply it to your finances. How can you reuse what you've already got to save money on buying new? How can you take the materials at your disposal and turn them into the things you need for survival?

First and foremost, always cook from scratch instead of choosing prepackaged. You're living on a homestead that should be full of the fruits of your labor literally! Why eat out or have food delivered when you have farm fresh goods right outside your door? The money you save on buying food when you are a homesteader is going to be your No. 1, biggest source of savings. You may not even realize how much money is spent on groceries and eating at restaurants until you give up on it altogether. That money can go towards better tools and equipment, better food and shelter for your animals, fixing up your kitchen, or any other of the many homesteading projects I'm sure you're just itching to take on soon.

Another great money-saving tip for homesteaders is DIY: Do it yourself. Nowadays, there are tutorials for just about anything accessible with the press of a button on your computer. You can make your own soaps, cleaning products, and even clothing! I definitely recommend learning how to knit or sew or even purchasing a sewing machine. They can be a little pricey, but worth it 100 times over if you use it right. Learning to mend ripped clothes or fix broken tools can save you a ton of money and time. Instead of shopping new, upcycle the old; try taking an old pair of jeans that no longer fit and turning them into shorts. Old clothing that is really unwearable can even be cut into strips and used as cleaning rags around the homestead. Remember, it's all about applying the mindset of sustainability to everything around you.

Finally, connect to your environment a little more. Instead of paying for television, movies, and other forms of entertainment to keep you occupied, try finding things to do that don't cost any money. Explore a new part of the area that you've never seen before, go for a swim in a nearby lake or river, take your animals on a walk outside the homestead, etc. There is such a huge and amazing world out there; you don't need to be cooped up inside all day! Borrow books from friends, neighbors, or even the local library instead of buying, and that way, when you finish, you can return them and they won't take up space cluttering up your home. Most importantly, remember to keep an open mind and always have your eyes peeled for new opportunities. There are always ways to improve and always new and exciting things to see and do.

MAKING MONEY

There are a variety of different ways to profit off the work you do on your homestead. Though you will most likely not be able to majorly profit immediately, with a steady work pace and consistent drive, you will break even and start earning an income in no time. A lot of the ways people make money on their homestead revolve around selling their goods. This means some extra work for preparing and packaging your foods or homemade goods, but you can sell at whatever price you set, as you will effectively be your own boss. Do some research, especially if you live nearby other homesteads or self-run businesses, and find out what's available in the market already and what there may be a greater need for in the future.

The best way to earn a profit from selling homemade or homegrown goods is to be consistent, reliable, and friendly. Making a name for yourself within your community can take some time, but don't give up. Get the word out and let people know what you have and how it can benefit them! You can even tell people that by buying from you, they are saving the planet by funding an eco-friendly business and a local food source.

As for what kinds of goods to sell, that's up to you. Of course, you can take your fresh produce directly to a farmers market, but you can also turn your crops into artisanal goods that will fetch a higher price. Selling homemade preserves like jam and honey, dried fruits or smoked meats, homemade cheese, herbs and spice mixes, and even homemade soaps and other cosmetics can all be very profitable if you know how to make them!

HOMEMADE JAM

Making your own jam is relatively easy, especially once you are used to all the hard work that comes with life on the homestead. Homemade jam crafted with organic fruits from your homestead can be a great way to start making money, as so many people love jam, and you can make all kinds of different flavors depending on what you've got at your disposal. Turning your fruits into jam also preserves them longer, so any ripe berries you may have that are about to go bad can easily be cooked up into a delicious jam that lasts. This way, you can store it longer for your own pantry, or sell to your friends, family, and local community.

Jam is super easy to make and only has a few simple steps. All you need is the fruit of your choice, some granulated sugar, and an acid juice of your choice. As a general rule, I like to use about ¼ to ⅔ of a cup of sugar for every pound of fruit. This comes out to about 52 to 130 grams of sugar for 450 grams of fruit. Now, depending on what fruit you are using, you may need to include a couple extra steps. If your fruit has a peel or skin, make sure to remove that as well as any pits. This step is necessary for fruits like peaches and plums. For the acid juice, you can use a freshly squeezed lemon or even lime, some white vinegar, or any other acidic juice of your choice. This is necessary to activate the fruits naturally occurring pectin, which is what makes jam thick and gel-like.

First, cut up your fruit into small pieces. They don't need to be exact as it will all be cooked together later. In a bowl, mix the sugar with your fruit, and stir it around with your hands to ensure that all the fruit pieces are fully and evenly covered. If you are a beginner, start by adding only a quarter cup of sugar. Afterwards, you can taste a piece of fruit and decide whether you want your jam sweeter or not. Once this is done, cover the bowl, and let it sit in the fridge for 24 hours. This step allows the fruit to break down properly and can help remove liquid which will better dissolve the sugar. After the fruit has macerated in the fridge for a day, transfer it into an appropriately-sized pot and bring to a boil on high heat. Once the mixture is boiling, add a couple teaspoons of your acid juice. I highly recommend using lemon juice for this step as it is organic and can possibly even be found on your own homestead. Reduce the heat to medium-low, and stir often to make sure the jam is even. At this point, you can add any herbs or aromatics you may want for some extra flavor, or use a potato masher to smooth out any chunks if you are going for a smooth-textured jam.

To check if your jam is finished cooking, you can do a "plate test". Spoon a small amount of the jam from the pot onto a plate. If the jam is still runny, it needs to cook for longer. Once the jam holds its blob form on the plate, that's how you will know it is done cooking. From here, you can transfer your jam into jars, let it cool, and then keep in the refrigerator for up to a month. If your goal is to sell your jam, you may want to consider using a canning technique to seal the jars so that they last longer for your customers.

When it comes to jam-making, a lot of the work is based on preference. If you want a smoother or chunkier jam, you can cut different-sized chunks of fruit and mash it up while simmering. You can also add multiple fruits if you want to make a mixed jam, though don't go overboard or you'll muddle the flavors. One trick I like to do when making my own jam is to strain it once it's finished cooking and before putting it in the jar. For berry jam, especially blackberry or raspberry, straining it will help remove any small seeds that I, personally, don't like to eat. Again, it is a preference thing and totally up to you and what kind of jam you want to make.

DRIED FRUITS

You already know how to dehydrate your fruits to make fruit leather; now it's time to package and sell! Dried fruits are especially good on-the-go snacks that can provide you with a delicious boost of energy while you are working, exercising, or just out and about. The trick to selling some good dried fruit or really *any* product from your homestead is good marketing and proper packaging. If you are homesteading in a rural area, it is more than likely that other homesteaders nearby will be doing *exactly* what you are doing, and trying to sell their goods. You need to make sure your product stands out, and let the people know exactly what they are supporting when they buy from you.

Dried fruit is durable and amenable, meaning pretty much any packaging will work as long as it is kept clean. You can use plastic bags or glass jars to wrap your dried fruits, and sell them individually or as a jumbled mix of all different flavors. When you sell your fruit, make sure to let customers know that they are making a difference by supporting you and your homestead, and be sure to tell them what goes into making these delicious goods. Giving customers some background information will help them feel more at ease purchasing from you, especially if they are a new customer. Sharing your stories may also influence them to try their hand at living more sustainably and may even persuade them to try homesteading. Something as simple as dried fruits can have a huge impact on your community and the planet.

One great way to get the word out about your homemade goods is to start a website. Building a website is super easy and cheap, and there are plenty of options available to help you find the perfect format and style for your site. Having an online shop where people can make purchases and have the goods shipped to them is a great way to expand your market outside of your local community. Make sure to put up some information about yourself and your homestead, as well as each product you want to sell. You should also always add clear, high quality photos of your products, so that people can see what it is they will be receiving when they make their purchase.

SELLING MEATS

The first thing you need to know about selling meat from your homestead is the laws and regulations that must be followed. In the United States, the only legal way to sell meat that has been homegrown on your homestead is to have it slaughtered and butchered at a USDA (United States Department of Agriculture) inspected processing facility. Livestock must be harvested and butchered onsite in order to be lawfully sold to a retailer, at a farmers market, to restaurants, etc. This is called a "retailer's cut". The advantages to this are that you can sell the meat individually packaged as opposed to selling the entire animal and make a premium, maximizing the profit you can make from your meat.

The only problem with going this route is that the processing fees from the facility can be hefty. On top of that, USDA inspectors are few and far between, meaning that you may have to drive a far distance just to get your meat processed properly.

This can seriously raise the costs and dissuade many homesteaders from going this route, as it may not be worth your while depending on how much meat you plan on selling. That's where the second option comes in, of course.

"Custom Butchery Exemption" is a way in which you can avoid going to a USDA-inspected facility; however, it is a little more complex and takes some extra work on your part. The details of this process are that you effectively sell the meat by selling the live animal wholesale and then make custom arrangements on behalf of the customer to get it custom butchered. "Custom meat" can include cattle, swine, sheep, or goat and does not need to be USDA-inspected when it is butchered. Custom meat is also legally only allowed to be used within the household by the owner. Thus, in order to follow the proper regulations, you need to make sure that your transaction is done for the *live animal*, not the meat itself. The transaction must be completed and ownership passed on to the customer, *prior* to the slaughter and butchery of the animal. Once the transaction is complete, you as the homesteader can have the butchering done on the customer's behalf.

Uninspected meat cannot be sold under any circumstances, so the butcher must mark the meat with a "Do Not Sell" label. This means that you limit your selling options, and the buyer of the animal must purchase and use all the meat themselves. Luckily, there are rules that allow for animals to be purchased by multiple buyers altogether. This means that cattle or larger animals can be divided into two or four pieces and sold to multiple consenting buyers. This method has advantages and disadvantages. As mentioned previously, you as the farmer will have to sell the meat in bulk, meaning the market for your product will be a lot smaller, and it may be hard to come by customers. The advantages are that you won't need to use a USDA-approved facility, meaning processing fees will certainly be a lot cheaper. Beyond that, the process will be less stressful for the animals as they won't have to endure the wait time and harsh conditions of a USDA-approved facility.

Selling meat can be tricky due to all the rules and regulations, so be careful and always do your research beforehand. Make sure you are fully aware of all the laws surrounding the selling and purchasing of live animals or butchered meat before making any commitments to customers, and if you are unsure about anything, it is always helpful to inquire with an inspector or official. You want your homestead to be successful, but not at the cost of breaking any food safety laws. These laws are in place for a reason; that mainly being the safety concerns surrounding food, particularly meats, and their preparation. If any of the processes between raising your animal to cooking your dinner are done incorrectly, or without proper health and safety measures, the food could be contaminated or unsafe for consumption. Always make sure you trust your butcher and anyone else who will be handling your livestock the same way you trust your waiter with your meal at a restaurant.

HERB AND SPICE MIXES

Creating your own mix of herbs or spice blends is super easy and fun! A lot of blends from the grocery store contain additives like MSG, so making homemade is actually healthier and can earn you a little income. All you need is the herbs and spices on your homestead, some small jars, and a little creativity. If you are going to sell individual spices, all you need is to package them up and add some labels. If you want to get a little fancy, though, making your own custom spice blends can be a great way to find a signature style for your homestead.

There are so many recipes available online for all different kinds of spice blends. Try to come up with some ideas based on what flavor profiles you like best, and then, experiment in your own kitchen to figure out what works well together. Obviously, you can go for some classics like an Italian or Mediterranean blend, but you can also make up your own combinations. Test out your spice combos at home with your family and even with your friends and peers. Once your test market aka your friends approve, get to bottling and selling!

One thing to remember with spice mixes is that people will probably want to try them out before purchasing, especially if you sell in a larger container. If you are selling at a farmers market or local shop, see if you can set up a sample tray. Add a little bit of spice mix to a small bowl with some olive oil and mix it up to create a dip, then allow people to try it out with pieces of bread or crackers. This will give them a good idea of the flavors without you having to cook up a bunch of homemade meals using all your spices.

CHICKEN EGGS

Selling your chicken eggs can be a great way to supplement your income and cover the cost of feed for your birds. Make sure to check the local laws and regulations regarding the sale of chicken eggs before you get started. You're also going to want to carefully clean the eggs before you sell them, as you and your family may not worry about some dirt on the shell, but customers might have a different opinion. The best way to keep your eggs clean is to keep the nesting boxes clean, so be sure to keep up with maintenance for your chickens each and every day.

Egg-sizing varies in some regions, but the general rule is that the size label increases every 0.25 ounces, starting at 1.25 oz for a peewee egg, 1.5 oz for a small, and going all the way to 2.5 oz for a jumbo. Now, proper sizing only has to be done for eggs that are going to be sold commercially, meaning to another vendor. If you just want to sell your eggs yourself with a stand or at a farmers market, you don't need to worry so much about the size. You can purchase plain egg cartons from a garden center or craft store, as you legally can't sell eggs in name brand cartons due to rules and rights surrounding branding. Make sure that when you sell your eggs you have a best before date on the carton as well!

One great tip for selling your homestead eggs is to raise chickens that lay different-colored eggs! Having a pop of color in those cartons can be very eye-catching and even exciting to buyers who generally shop at the grocery store and may only be used to white and brown eggs. You should also always give your customer details on how your chickens are raised. People will often be willing to spend a little more money on their food if they know it has been made sustainably and that the animals are happy and well cared for, of course.

HARVESTING HONEY AND BEESWAX

If you've decided to house a bee colony on your homestead, selling the honey and beeswax can fetch you a pretty penny. Beeswax has so many purposes; it's great for candles, polishing wood or leather, cosmetic use, arts and crafts, and so much more! Not to mention that fresh, locally-sourced honey is very on trend these days.

Beeswax can be sold both locally and commercially to individuals in the community and businesses alike. Many businesses use beeswax to make other products and having a good supplier is always necessary. If your apiary is large enough, you can definitely find some larger corporations that look for wholesale suppliers like you! Selling at local fairs, farmers markets, and even just from your own porch is another way to earn some income and grow your customer base. Whether you sell the beeswax in sheets or in the form of some other craft you've created, people will love these homestead goods.

Honey is great for local consumers, farmers markets, and even local restaurants or grocery stores. Many smaller businesses may be seeking to find locally-sourced ingredients for their own business recipes, and that's where you come into the picture. Providing a local cafe with fresh honey for their pastries and coffees can be a sweet deal (no pun intended) and gain you a reputation as a notable seller in your community.

Soapmaking and Cosmetics

Natural, homemade soap is another great way to earn an income on your homestead. Making your own soap is also relatively simple and can be done right from your kitchen. All you need to make homemade soap is lye, water, solid oils, liquid oils, and your scents. The scents can come from essential oils or any aromatics you may have growing on your homestead. You can also choose to add color to your soaps as well as extra decor like pressed flowers or seeds within the mix. There are plenty of recipes for easy homemade soaps available online, and most of them are super simple and easy to follow.

The simplest of soap recipes contain only six ingredients; 16 ounces of coconut oil, 14 ounces of palm oil, 21 ounces of olive oil, 19 ounces of distilled water, a two pound container of lye, and seven or so teaspoons of the essential oil of your choice (or any other ingredient you want to use for scent). This amount will provide you with enough for four full batches of soap. The first step is to put on some rubber gloves because handling lye can be harmful to your skin before it is properly mixed. Carefully measure 200 grams of lye and 19 ounces of distilled water, and then, mix the two together in a glass pitcher, stirring just long enough for all the lye to dissolve. The chemical reaction that ensues will cause the solution to heat up and release fumes; this is totally normal. Let the solution cool for about an hour before you continue.

Next step is to prepare your mold and measure out your fragrance. You can use one scent or combine multiple in different amounts, as long as you make sure that you are measuring out seven teaspoons of essential oils. Then, you are going to melt and mix all the oils, including the coconut, palm, and olive oils. Since some of these are solid at room temperature, you will need to melt them down before adding them. Once your lye mixture and your oils all reach the same temperature range of about 80 to 100-degrees, blend them together in a large pot. Always add the lye mixture to the oils and not the other way around. The mixture should turn cloudy, and continue to blend for about three or four minutes. You are aiming for the consistency of a runny pudding or melted jello, and once you reach this consistency, slowly and evenly mix in your fragrance or essential oils.

After that, all that's left is to pour the mixture carefully into your molds. Then, let it cool in the fridge or outside for at least 24 hours before removing it. Your soap can then be removed and cut into sizes of your preference. When cleaning up, make sure you scrub everything down properly. I recommend that you don't use any of the tools that interacted with the lye for any other purpose, as trace amounts may remain even after thorough cleaning.

WORMS

One thing you may not have thought of when coming up with profitable homestead projects is raising and selling worms! As you know, worms are great for soil composition, compost, and so much more. They are an essential part of agriculture and homestead living. So, why not take this essential part of your life and make some money off of it?

Worms reproduce extremely rapidly and have so many benefits. Soil improvement, compost production, and even fishing! There are always people looking to buy worms, which seems silly because they live in the ground just about everywhere. Depending on how large you want to grow your worm business and how much space you have on your homestead, you're going to want to take a relatively large bin and fill it with soil. Next, make sure you have lots and lots of feedstock for your worms. This could be anything from animal manure to dried leaves and plants to shredded newspapers. Worms love to eat all kinds of organic materials. Once you introduce the worms to the bin, make sure to keep the environment comfortable for them. Worms thrive in warm, moist places, so keep your soil in a dark and warm place, adding water as often as necessary.

When worms breed, they secrete a cocoon that can contain any number of eggs between one and about 20, depending on the species. Over the spring, worms may continue to mate every three or four days throughout the entire season, producing so many baby worms that you won't know what to do with them! Once they hatch, you can gather up your worms and package them in small containers with enough nutrient-dense soil to keep them happy and fat when you sell. Worms are generally sold at a price by the pound, so find a container to package them with this in mind.

You can then sell your worms commercially to large agriculture corporations that may be in need or locally to farmers and fishers in your community. My own father loves fishing, and when I was young, I used to always beg him to buy me an extra bucket of worms so that I could raise a little worm family in the backyard. Maybe it was an early sign that I would be a homesteader, or maybe I was just a silly child. Either way, I never got my worms until I grew up and started raising them myself.

HOST EVENTS

One last idea for making a profit on your homestead is to host events! Homesteads and farms can be great venues for parties and celebrations such as weddings, community events, and even educational trips for businesses and schools. Your homestead can be a great scenic location for important moments in other people's lives.

Hosting celebrations like weddings can be a great way to supplement your income if you've got the space and supplies. Plus, your duties as the venue are relatively simple. You can hire people to set up beforehand and clean up afterwards or negotiate a contract in which that is the guest's responsibility. Either way, people will pay a lot to have their wedding or other celebration in the perfect spot, and a homestead is the perfect combination of rustic, outdoorsy, and scenic! Especially if you are growing colorful plants and flowers that act as built-in decor, hosting parties and events on your property can be a great way to make some money and introduce new people to homesteading and any other products you may be selling.

Hosting academic events like a school field trip can also be a great way to teach children about the joys and hardships of homesteading. Schools are always looking for new ways to get kids interested in learning and keep them entertained. Your homestead is the perfect location for them to learn all about homegrown food, hard work ethic, and sustainable living. You can help kids grow up to be passionate, empowered, eco-warriors who may even start their own homesteads one day; all of this, while also getting paid for hosting!

Running activities and events for community members or even corporate retreats is another great idea. Hard work on a farm is exactly what so many businesses are in need of when they are searching for team-building exercises that can increase company morale and build strong work ethic. Plus, living on a beautiful homestead for a night or two is a perfect little mini vacation for most city people, even if they do have to work all day.

Talk to your local community event organizers, such as public officials and community center staff, to find out more about how your homestead can be used for public events and activities. Even a small homestead can be useful for community-run events like outdoor movie nights, cooking classes, and so much more. Plus, this is a great way to become closer to your neighbors and peers. You can make friends, get more people interested in the homestead lifestyle, and even grow your customer base for many of your products. Additionally, for any of these events, you can always have a little stand set up with other goods you are selling like your jams or chicken eggs. That way, not only will you profit from hosting the events, but you can also earn a nice bonus from visitors who want to bring home a souvenir.

CONCLUSION

Congratulations! You've made it to the end of the guide, and you've successfully educated yourself on all the basics of a good homestead. What comes next is up to you. Do you want to start raising chickens in your backyard? Or maybe you are going to start a little vegetable garden? Maybe, you even feel confident enough to start running a full homestead, top to bottom? Whatever your decision, we at Small Footprint Press are proud of you for making it this far and learning all the tricks to sustainable homestead living.

We hope that this guidebook helped you to not only learn the basics of how to live on a homestead, but also taught you the importance of why you *should*. We are all responsible for the well-being of this planet, and living in a capitalist, consumption-based society is simply not sustainable anymore; in fact, it never *was*. We need to collectively shift away from a consumer mindset and become producers of our own needs and wants if we are going to truly make progress towards taking better care of the earth. It is your responsibility, just as much as the next person, to ensure a happy, healthy, and safe place from which future generations can benefit. Living the homesteader lifestyle is just the beginning.

You've learned how to prepare yourself mentally and physically for homesteading. You've learned about growing crops and raising animals. You've also learned about making things from scratch, building shelters and sheds, preserving food and materials for later use, and even how to expand your wealth and share with your community. Now it is time for you to take this knowledge and put it to good use. All this reading will have been for nothing if you don't go out and start living more sustainably today.

If you take even just one lesson away from this, let it be that your mindset is the most important tool at your disposal. You truly can do anything you put your mind to so long as you believe in yourself, work hard, and never give up. It may sound cheesy, but it is nothing but the truth. Just go online and look up how many successful homesteaders are sharing their stories. It is possible to live sustainably, to grow and serve your own food, and to prepare for the worst and expect the best. Everything we've talked about throughout this entire book is possible for you, as long as you put your mind to it.

Shifting your mindset can be hard work, but it is absolutely crucial, especially in this day and age. If we want to leave this world a better place than we found it, we must all do our share to restore and revive Mother Nature through sustainable, agricultural practices, proper recycling and reusing of materials and resources, and actively working towards 100 percent sustainability. You may not be able to get there right away in fact, it would be impossible to try but we can all get there eventually. Homesteading wherever you live is possible!

When it comes to homesteading, or even just simple gardening, the work you put in is what you will see in return. The more work you put into your homestead, the better it will be and the better you will feel. It is a difficult task, yes, and it takes a lot of energy, effort, and commitment, but done properly, it is so worth it. Your homegrown food will taste a million times better even just knowing that you made it completely yourself and in an environmentally-conscious fashion. Plus, the satisfaction and fulfillment you will feel when you finally eat that first bite; that alone is worth all the fast food in the world!

There you have it—all the knowledge you need to start your homestead, right in your very own backyard. Now that you've finished reading and researching, it's time to get to work. Whether it be on a huge plot of farmland, in your suburban backyard, or even just on your front porch, you can start living the homesteader life today!

REFERENCES

5 steps to homestead success and a winning mindset. (2012, November 28). Joybilee® Farm | DIY | Herbs | Gardening |. https://joybileefarm.com/5-steps-to-homestead-abundance/

7 Easy Steps to Composting | City of Leduc. (2019). Leduc.ca. https://www.leduc.ca/composting/7-easy-steps-composting

7 Tips to Help You Sell Your Farm Fresh Eggs For More Money. (n.d.). Fresh Eggs Daily®. https://www.fresheggsdaily.blog/2017/05/7-tips-to-help-you-sell-your-farm-fresh.html

8 Ways to Build a More Sustainable Homestead. (2020, June 28). Kaits Garden. https://kaitsgarden.com/2020/06/27/8-ways-to-build-a-more-sustainable-homestead/

9 Ways to Stay Grounded in Uncertain Times | Coping With COVID-19 | Stamford Health. (n.d.). Www.stamfordhealth.org. https://www.stamfordhealth.org/healthflash-blog/infectious-disease/9-ways-to-stay-grounded/

11 Ways to Stick to Your Budget. (n.d.). Www.valleyfirst.com. https://www.valleyfirst.com/simple-advice/money-advice/ways-to-stick-to-your-budget

admin, & admin. (2019, July 27). *A Complete Guide to Solar Electric Fences: Build an Off-Grid Fence.* Greencoast.org. https://greencoast.org/solar-electric-fence/

Avery, J. (2018, January 8). *How To Stay Committed To Reaching Your Goals.* Farm Homestead. https://farmhomestead.com/how-to-stay-committed-to-reaching-your-goals/

Basic Chicken Keeping Hints & Tips | Chicken Houses & Coops | Poultry Supplies. (n.d.). Www.flytesofancy.co.uk. https://www.flytesofancy.co.uk/chickenhouses/basic_chicken_keeping.html

Benefits of Composting. (n.d.). Less Is More. https://lessismore.org/materials/72-benefits-of-composting/

Careta, M. (2015, June 8). *The 5 Most Important Crops You Need For Survival.* Off the Grid News.

https://www.offthegridnews.com/survival-gardening-2/the-5-most-important-crops-you-need-for-survival/

Carleo, J. (2017, January). *FS1263: Ultra-Niche Crop Series: Writing SMART Goals for Your Farm (Rutgers NJAES)*. Njaes.rutgers.edu. https://njaes.rutgers.edu/fs1263/

Charbonneau, J. (2017, February 3). *33 Homestead Plants that are Easy to Grow*. Survival Sullivan. https://www.survivalsullivan.com/33-easy-grow-plants-homestead-prepper/

Doval, C. (2018, December 11). *What is Sustainable Agriculture?* Sustainable Agriculture Research & Education Program. https://sarep.ucdavis.edu/sustainable-ag

familydoctor.org editorial staff. (2010, May). *Changing Your Diet: Choosing Nutrient-rich Foods - familydoctor.org*. Familydoctor.org. https://familydoctor.org/changing-your-diet-choosing-nutrient-rich-foods/

Flottum, K. (2015, January 29). *Beekeeping 101: Supplies, Plans and How To*. Popular Mechanics. https://www.popularmechanics.com/home/lawn

-garden/how-to/g56/diy-backyard-beekeeping-47031701/

Great Benefits of Homesteading. (2014, January 21). The Elliott Homestead. https://theelliotthomestead.com/2014/01/great-benefits-of-homesteading/

Harvard Health Publishing. (2019, February 6). *The best foods for vitamins and minerals - Harvard Health.* Harvard Health. https://www.health.harvard.edu/staying-healthy/the-best-foods-for-vitamins-and-minerals

History.com Editors. (2018, August 21). *Homestead Act.* HISTORY. https://www.history.com/topics/american-civil-war/homestead-act

Home Wind Power: Yes, in My Backyard! | MOTHER EARTH NEWS. (2014). Mother Earth News. https://www.motherearthnews.com/renewable-energy/wind-power/home-wind-power-zm0z13amzrob

Homestead exemption. (2021, February 2). Wikipedia. https://en.wikipedia.org/wiki/Homestead_exemption

Homestead Exemption Rules and Regulations. (n.d.). Www.dor.ms.gov.
https://www.dor.ms.gov/Pages/Homestead-Rules.aspx

Homestead Goats - What You Need to Know to Get Started. (2016, December 9). Common Sense Home.
https://commonsensehome.com/homestead-goats/

Housing Your Chickens: All You Need to Know to Do It Properly. (2018, December 20). MorningChores.
https://morningchores.com/chicken-housing/

How Does Solar Power Work | Solar Power Experts. (n.d.). Infinite Energy.
https://www.infiniteenergy.com.au/about-solar-power/how-solar-power-works/

How Does Solar Work? (n.d.). Energy.gov.
https://www.energy.gov/eere/solar/how-does-solar-work

How to Build a Raised Bed CHEAP and EASY, Backyard Gardening. (n.d.). Www.youtube.com.
https://www.youtube.com/watch?app=desktop&v=MBIYebUgVVI

How to Install Outdoor Electric Wiring. (n.d.). WikiHow. https://www.wikihow.com/Install-

Outdoor-Electric-Wiring

How to Make Soap at Home (Even if You Failed Chemistry). (2020, August 12). Food52. https://food52.com/blog/12919-how-to-make-soap-at-home-even-if-you-failed-chemistry

How to Sell Backyard Chicken Eggs. (2017, May 8). The Happy Chicken Coop. https://www.thehappychickencoop.com/how-to-sell-backyard-chicken-eggs/

How to Sell Meat Legally as Part of Your Homestead Business. (n.d.). www.youtube.com. https://www.youtube.com/watch?app=desktop&v=IxO9GweZDEM

How to Sell Your Honey and Beeswax Harvest. (2019, August 11). MorningChores. https://morningchores.com/how-to-sell-honey-and-beeswax/

How to Stay Grounded and Centered in Life: 6 Techniques. (2020, June 6). Put the Kettle On.

https://putthekettleon.ca/how-to-stay-grounded-and-centered-in-life/

How to stretch a fence. (n.d.). Www.youtube.com. https://www.youtube.com/watch?app=desktop&v=tkSPejY7g-U

Hydroponics at Home. (n.d.). Www.youtube.com. https://www.youtube.com/watch?app=desktop&v=1oETmA6AJQk

Jan 30, F. | H. 3040 | U., & Print, 2020 |. (2020, January 30). *Canning Foods at Home.* Home & Garden Information Center | Clemson University, South Carolina. https://hgic.clemson.edu/factsheet/canning-foods-at-home/

Krista, A. (2020, August 15). *Dehydrating Foods for Storage: An Essential Homesteading Skill.* Goose Creek Homestead. https://goosecreekhomestead.com/dehydrating-foods-for-storage/

Leigh. (n.d.). *Mindset: Key To Successful Homesteading?* 5 Acres and a Dream. https://www.5acresandadream.com/2011/01/mindset-key-to-successful-homesteading.html

Link, R. (2017). *The 14 Healthiest Vegetables on Earth.* Healthline. https://www.healthline.com/nutrition/14-healthiest-vegetables-on-earth

Lovely Greens. (2013, September 20). Lovely Greens. https://lovelygreens.com/natural-soapmaking-for-beginners/

Makena, W. (n.d.). *How to succeed in the dried fruits business.* The Standard. https://www.standardmedia.co.ke/hustle/article/2001324409/how-to-succeed-in-the-dried-fruits-business

Making Soil Blocks. (n.d.). Www.youtube.com. https://www.youtube.com/watch?app=desktop&v=xLbAkqau_MI

McCoy, D. (2019, November 25). *10 Essential Crops for a Self Sufficient Garden.* The Rustic Elk. https://www.therusticelk.com/self-sufficient-garden/

Mubitana, S. (2017, December 8). *How to Start a Dried Fruits Business.* Smatfin. https://smatfin.com/how-to-start-a-dried-fruits-business/

North, D. (2016, May 30). *What is Aquaponics and How Does it Work?* The Permaculture Research Institute. https://www.permaculturenews.org/2016/05/30/what-is-aquaponics-and-how-does-it-work/

Reynolds, M. (n.d.). *Build a Backyard Bee House.* DIY. https://www.diynetwork.com/how-to/outdoors/gardening/build-a-backyard-bee-house

seamsterFollow. (n.d.). *Build a Simple Shed: a Complete Guide.* Instructables. Retrieved https://www.instructables.com/Build-a-simple-shed-a-complete-guide/

Self-watering SIP Sub-irrigated Raised Bed Construction (How to Build). (2015, April 29). Www.youtube.com. https://www.youtube.com/watch?app=desktop&v=Lp9Jdyno9hI

Setting a fence post. (n.d.). Www.youtube.com. https://www.youtube.com/watch?app=desktop&v=9D2H_xq78Mw

Smoking Meat 101 - [Complete Guide] Smoking & Types of Smokers. (2018, March 7). Smoking Meat Geeks | #MeatGeeks.

163

https://smokingmeatgeeks.com/smoking-meat-basics/

Superstore, R. (n.d.). *Re-roof your shed roof: A DIY Guide*. Roofing Superstore Help & Advice. https://www.roofingsuperstore.co.uk/help-and-advice/product-guides/pitched-roofing/reroof-your-shed-roof/

Tamara, N. (n.d.). *50 Essential Crops to Grow in Your Survival Garden*. Https://Crisisequipped.com/. https://crisisequipped.com/crops-to-grow-in-your-survival-garden/

The Easiest Way To Make Any Homemade Fruit Jam (feat. Krewella). (n.d.). Www.youtube.com. https://www.youtube.com/watch?app=desktop&v=KUGjgUA-BWU

Top 10 Homestead Crops. (2020, December 4). Mary's Heirloom Seeds. https://www.marysheirloomseeds.com/blogs/news/top-10-homestead-crops

verticalroots. (2020, March 3). *What is hydroponic farming? Why use hydroponics?* Vertical Roots. https://www.verticalroots.com/the-what-and-why-of-hydroponic-farming/

Vivian, J. (n.d.). *The Secrets of Low-Tech Plumbing.* Mother Earth News. https://www.motherearthnews.com/homesteading-and-livestock/low-tech-plumbing-zmaz95jjztak

We've Broken Down the Science of Composting for You. (n.d.). Better Homes & Gardens. https://www.bhg.com/gardening/yard/compost/how-to-compost/

What is Aquaponics. (2019). The Aquaponic Source. https://www.theaquaponicsource.com/what-is-aquaponics/

Why You Should Have Goats on Your Homestead. (n.d.). Oak Hill Homestead. https://www.oakhillhomestead.com/2014/03/why-you-should-have-goats-on-your.html

Winger, J. (2015, January 2). *7 Reasons to Start Homesteading Today.* The Prairie Homestead. https://www.theprairiehomestead.com/2015/01/start-homesteading-today.html